CHOICES →WITH← CLOUT

How to Make Things Happen— by Making the Right Decisions Every Day of Your Life

WILBUR CROSS

BERKLEY BOOKS, NEW YORK

CHOICES WITH CLOUT

A Berkley Book / published by arrangement with
Wilbur Cross Associates, Inc.

PRINTING HISTORY
Berkley edition / January 1995

ISBN: 0-425-14538-7

BERKLEY®
Berkley Books are published by The Berkley Publishing Group,
200 Madison Avenue, New York, New York 10016.
BERKLEY and the "B" design
are trademarks belonging to Berkley Publishing Corporation.

PRINTED IN THE UNITED STATES OF AMERICA

10 9 8 7 6 5 4 3 2

Contents

CONTENTS

Dedicated to
the memory of my grandfather,
Wilbur Lucious Cross,
a noted scholar and governor of Connecticut,
who made some unique choices in life
that led him down the pathways
of four distinctive and distinguished careers
as teacher, author, editor, and statesman

Foreword

I first met Jay Van Andel and Rich DeVos in 1984, when I was commissioned to coauthor the official history of the Amway Corporation, which was published by the Benjamin Company in 1986 under the title *Commitment to Excellence*. While engaged in this project, I was greatly inspired by the personal philosophies of Rich and Jay and proposed that they author a motivational book for general readers. Although they modestly declined the proposal, they did give me a green light to read through their numerous writings, listen to their speeches, interview them at great length, and eventually publish the proposed book under my own byline. This work is the result of that extensive research, over for an entire decade, from 1984 to 1994.

Among the contributors to the company history was former President Gerald R. Ford, a longtime friend of Rich and Jay, and a firm believer in their personal philosophies and business policies. He authored the Foreword for the book, in which he said of the two Amway founders, "I have known both of them for many years, going back to the days when I was a United States Congressman from Michigan. I have watched their business grow and spread from our home state right across the United States, north into Canada, and around the world. I have taken a deep personal interest in their accomplishments. More importantly, I have been proud of the way in which their company has become one of the prime representatives of the free enterprise system in many lands and among many peoples.

"The thousands of Amway distributorships are dramatic proof that the American spirit of free enterprise is, and will continue to be, a vibrant force at home and abroad. Each of them is, in effect, an ambassador earning respect and support for the democratic way of life . . . I can only say to Rich and Jay that I hope they go on forever, attracting the peoples of the world to a better way of life and bringing new hope for the future."

Preface

We first met Wilbur Cross in 1984, when we were looking for a top-ranking professional writer to author the official history of the Amway Corporation. Cross's endeavors resulted in a splendid book, *Commitment to Excellence,* which was published by the Benjamin Company in 1986 and has been an inspiration for thousands of readers ever since.

Shortly after completing this work, Wilbur Cross came to us with the proposal that we consider authoring a motivational type of book that would introduce and portray our philosophies of life. As he expressed it, we had helped many thousands of people along the road to success in our business operations, and we could multiply the message many times over to an even greater audience of people all around the world through the pages of the proposed book.

He offered to act as the editor and assist us in selecting and organizing the wealth of material we had composed in the form of articles, speeches, tape recordings, films, and other media. Intrigued by the idea, we not only compiled an overwhelming collection of such materials, but agreed to four lengthy interviews, during which we explored all aspects of the subject. Later, because of the pressures of community service and business commitments, we decided that Cross should author the book, based on our manifold discussions and documentation. We felt, furthermore, that an outside author could present the material in a more objective manner than we could, and would relieve us of asserting what we believed with great conviction while avoiding the impression that we were trying to preach.

Wilbur Cross has our blessing in this endeavor, as well as our heartfelt confidence that the message will benefit the largest possible audience of readers, both in America and abroad.

—Jay Van Andel and Rich DeVos

Introduction

"Hitch Your Wagon to a Star."

This romantic bit of advice about making a vital choice that would forever affect your life and future was popular in the nineteenth century, from a work by the noted poet, Robert Browning.

Then it faded from popularity. WHY?

Because it became OLD HAT. Wagons no longer created images of people who were really going somewhere significant.

Yet the innate truth remains. If you want to go places and be successful, choose the *right vehicle* to carry you to the destination you have decided is the right one for you.

It may be a deep-sea submarine. Or a rocket to the stars.

Look beyond the commonplace and tap your inspiration from things that are not earthbound, conventional, or plodding.

What does the quotation have in common with:

- An American saying, "You are what you eat"
- The title of a book, *The Power of Positive Thinking*
- An ancient Chinese proverb, "Life is partly what we make it and partly what is made by the friends we choose"

The answer is that they are all based on
THE INDIVIDUAL'S POWER OF CHOICE

We grow fat or thin, healthy or sickly through our choice of the foods we select to eat.

We develop a more powerful self by choosing books and other reading matter that focus on positive and provocative subjects.

We shape our life and lifestyle not only through our own doing but under the influence of the people with whom we choose to associate.

Putting the ideas in perspective, they all add up to one innate truth:

CHOICE IS AN ALL-IMPORTANT FACTOR IN
OUR LIVES,
A KEY TO SUCCESS, HAPPINESS, AND
PERSONAL ACHIEVEMENT

What about all those other factors that are important and that have been cited again and again by people who are successful or who have achieved certain objectives? People who possess qualities like motivation and perseverance and energy?

The answer is that they are *vital to personal success,* but they are also directly *dependent upon personal choice.*

The MOST IMPORTANT ASPECT OF MOTIVATION is the choice of people you associate with. In the case of young people, the motivation can start with parents who encourage their sons and daughters to cultivate the right friends and associates.

- Successful parents *take the initiative.*
- Successful parents *continually pursue* this goal.

BUT DON'T BE FOOLED OR MISLED.

Peer pressure is probably going to be *the dominant factor* in making choices.

The same is true of adults. No matter how motivated a person may be, that motivation is going to be

strengthened or w e a k e n e d

by the person's choice of friends and associates.

The nature and character of your own friends and close associates are factors that are eventually going to shape

- Your attitudes about life
- Your evaluation of careers
- Your vision of lifestyles
- Your judgment about what you can accomplish in life

Children who are born into a doctor's family—to use a common example—are likely to assume that they, too, *could* be doctors, if they wished to be. If one of your parents is a doctor at the time you are trying to shape your future career, it is natural for you to be confident that you, too, could become a doctor.

You might not feel the same confidence about aspiring to be a lawyer, going into banking, or becoming an airline pilot. Yet the offspring of lawyers and bankers and pilots would think nothing of aiming for those fields, if so inclined.

Young people who live in an atmosphere of a certain level of accomplishment grow up believing themselves suited for

THAT SAME LEVEL OF ACCOMPLISHMENT

even though they may in the end choose to select a completely different field.

ON THE OTHER SIDE OF THE COIN,

children who grow up in households where the parental levels of education are low are likely to be dubious about their own ability to succeed in college or along higher educational levels.

Educated parents almost invariably *take it for granted* that their sons and daughters will want to—and will have the talents to—follow in their footsteps, educationally at least. This kind of *positive* opinion leads to *positive* outlooks in the young themselves.

Success Through One's Choice of Association

That idea extends beyond families, friends, and associates to less animate areas that are also symbolic of success. These include

- *The church*
- *The community*
- *The nation*

and even *intangible concepts* that are positive forces in the lives of people of all ages and in all places.

The purpose of this short book is to **help you learn how to make those choices that will guide you to the people, institutions, concepts, and methods that are undeniably associated with success in the finest and most effective interpretation of the word.**

If you *associate* yourself with success, if you choose to *tap the roots* of things successful, if you *think* in terms of achievement, then you, too, will attain your goal—and even beyond that immediate target, you will reach goals that you never dreamed were within your range.

Even in an age of rockets and spacecraft and exploring vehicles that aim their sights at the fringes of the universe, it is never old hat and outdated to say to yourself,

"HITCH YOUR WAGON TO A STAR."

CHOICES →WITH← CLOUT

CHAPTER

1

The Rewards of Making the Right Choices

"The strongest principle of growth lies in human choice."

—George Eliot

NOTE TO THE READER

Throughout the book, there are sections headed **SELF STARTER,** to help you develop your own thoughts and actions as you proceed, specifically in conjunction with the book's theories and recommendations. The objective of each motivational passage is to stimulate your responsiveness and participation.

These **S/S** exercises are explored, too, in greater detail, in the Appendix to the book, on pages 183 to 190.

Shortly after World War II, upon being discharged from military service, Rich DeVos and Jay Van Andel made two choices that would affect their entire lives and the lives of many people who were close to them. They made those choices jointly, and hence with about twice the degree of difficulty that would have been needed for a single unequivocal choice.

The first choice, reached independently, was that they would go into business for themselves rather than enter the corporate world as employees.

The second was that they would go into partnership in whatever ventures and enterprises they decided looked promising for future growth and development. As it turned out, both choices were sound and have long since resulted in personal fulfillment and professional achievement beyond even their most optimistic dreams, not only for them but for literally hundreds of thousands of people who, over the years, have chosen to cast their lot with them in their particular endeavors.

What kind of magic were they talking about? You won't believe it, but

- They did not conceive some unique kind of business no one had ever concocted before.
- They did not work out some surprisingly innovative plan of action.
- They did not start off on the road to success in high gear with power-play economic support from an interested "angel."

Quite the opposite. They first tried their hand at a number of joint ventures that lacked the growth potential they had so optimistically envisioned, including the formation of a flying school and the opening of a drive-in restaurant. These were both moderately successful and might have provided a rewarding and comfortable living for a handful of participants. But they led to something much bigger, and what mattered most was that DeVos and Van Andel chose to be persistent. They persisted in the endeavors they had chosen. They persisted in dreaming the dream. And they persisted in refuting the prophets of doom who kept warning them about the ogre of insolvency lurking down the road.

Soon, as they wrestled with the many unfamiliar problems of keeping their restaurant venture properly supplied, they became involved in the distribution of a line of food supplements. Although there were numerous setbacks and limitations, they perceived great hope for the concept of using this widespread distributor system that they had been formulating. This led to the birth of Amway. What was Amway? Linguistically, it was their abbreviation for The American Way. Generically, it was a symbol of free enterprise. Commercially, it was the marketing of a unique line of consumer products, backed by the conviction that they had finally zeroed in on the business in which both of their futures would lie.

That enterprise had its origins at the end of the 1950s. Today, looking back on more than three decades of successful growth and development, they are often asked to pinpoint those qualities and beliefs that are essential to personal goals and achievements and that elusive quality known as success.

Their first response is always to ask the question, "What do you mean by success?"

SELF STARTER

Before you read farther, jot down what you consider success to be in your own life.

Choosing Your Own Version of Success

The word *success* denotes many things to many people, so we can only talk about our own interpretations. For each of us, success has many dimensions, including

- Personal fulfillment
- The realization of a dream
- The satisfaction of being able to share our hopes, aspirations, and accomplishments with other people
- The chance to relieve ourselves of long-standing complexities in society and live simpler lives

Success is not simply the attainment of goals that are material, but those that are *psychological, cultural, emotional,* and often *spiritual* as well.

What Is the Purpose of This Book?

In the chapters and sections and exercises that make up this volume, the focus is on the philosophies of relationships and living and working—the rationale and outlook that have enabled DeVos and Van Andel, as well as multitudes of people who have followed their advice, to achieve the goals they defined. The principles presented in this book are based not on intellectual theories alone but on many years of persistence, trial and error, and the resolve that they would attain the objectives that they had established for themselves, individually and as lifetime partners in ongoing enterprises of many kinds. While you may not agree with all of their concepts, I assure you that these principles have worked not only for DeVos and Van Andel, but also for their families, friends, and for hundreds of thousands of people around the world who have learned how to live lives that are

- Richer
- More fulfilling
- Happier
- And more rewarding in every way

With this in mind, the principles presented here can show *any* reader who really desires to improve how to achieve success in the best sense of the word. That's why the text is interspersed with self-help exercises like the following:

SELF STARTER

To condition yourself to choose positive outlooks, ask yourself this simple question: *"How many people do I know who feel that their lives are constantly being controlled by circumstances?"*

Very quickly, you will realize that most people feel this way to a greater or lesser degree. Yet they are living under a misconception. *Almost everyone has the opportunity and the option to make choices.* Many people tend to feel that they are powerless:

- They have too many children
- Or too little money
- Or not enough education
- Or the competition is too stiff

One thing or another is always against them. Looking around your circle of friends and relatives, you can easily think of other "pitfalls" that generate this attitude. These negative thinkers tend to become afraid to try for something better, and eventually they simply give up.

Despite the prevalence of this attitude, most of us in any normal level of society have three vital assets:*

- The *power* to choose
- The *ability* to choose
- The *right* to choose

*We address the first asset here and the other two in following chapters.

The Power to Choose

Do you have a *"fix-it"* mentality that makes plans for dealing with a problem? Or do you have a *"woe is me"* outlook, which laments that the cards are always stacked against you? Many people go through life without ever being conscious of making choices.

They attend a certain school like everyone else they know.
They hang around with the same old pals, all engaged in the same business or avocation.
Their parents push them in a certain direction, much as they themselves had been pushed.
They have the same recreational pursuits as those they know and take the same kinds of vacations.

For these people, the various functions of living seem willy-nilly, just to happen. But look at it this way: Every single day, every hour, almost every minute, you are making choices of one kind or another. Though some are important and some insignificant, they are all choices.

- Will you buy this or that car model?
- Stay in this job or look for a different one?
- Attend a religious service or remain at home?
- Eat a big meal or a light one?
- Make a phone call or put it off?
- Read a book or watch TV?
- Stay on the main road or try a shortcut?
- Retire or keep on working?

SELF STARTER

Think of some choices you recently had the power to make. Jot them down in the order of significance. Then list them again in the order of difficulty required to make the final decision.

For any given individual, such a list is virtually endless, continuing merrily along from one day to the next and stretching into weeks, months, and years. Eventually, the combined impact of all these choices—even the seemingly minor ones—leads people down one road or another.

What really are the consequences of having made a particular decision, having gone in one direction instead of another? Each one of us can look back on his or her life and come up with answers. In the case of Rich DeVos and Jay Van Andel, they said they made a choice one day when they were in their late teens that was seemingly quite insignificant. Instead of finding separate means of transportation to school, they decided to share the ride. That simple choice, a mere matter of convenience, led to their becoming fast friends. And shortly that friendship (as already recounted) led to their going into business together—fortunately, with great success.

But what would have happened if they had made a different choice and had never gotten together? Their lives would have been totally different. The impact of that small—unbelievably small—choice has affected not only their careers but practically every aspect of their lives: marriage, family, travel and recreation, and relationships in the community. In short, everything that has been important to them and those they care about and love.

SELF STARTER

Think about just one small choice in your own life that led to a much more significant choice, perhaps in one of the categories mentioned above. Did you meet your spouse-to-be because you went to a football weekend instead of a fishing trip? Did you select your style of residence because you read a certain magazine instead of another? Did you end up with a job in Atlanta instead of San Francisco because you met someone at a social event who gave you a likely contact?

Do the Right Choices Guarantee Satisfaction?

Of course not!

All human beings encounter difficulties as they travel down the road they choose. It is not the difficulties that matter so much but the ways you hurdle these roadblocks that determine how far and how meaningfully you will progress. "When we started out to develop a career," says DeVos, "we could very easily have spent time griping about the fact that we got caught up in World War II and had to spend several years in military service. Quite frankly, though, we simply were too eager to get on with our lives to waste time fretting. From the beginning of our joint venture, we were energized by the challenge of making decisions and acting upon them. So, quite without realizing it, we automatically made choices: here were the things we wanted to do, and here was the outlook we'd take."

SELF STARTER

List at least two roadblocks in life you have successfully hurdled. List two others you have not yet hurdled, or that you failed to leapfrog in the past. How have the results affected your life?

To move forward in life, you need to focus your attention on what you should be doing and what you need to accomplish, rather than sulking about having somehow been dealt an unfair hand of cards. This hardly implies that you can control the shuffle. But when adversity strikes, you will make better decisions if you have established the habit of being decisive. By contrast, if you have never been able to make up your mind or if you sidestep minor agreements, then you are poorly conditioned to deal with the major decisions that inevitably surface.

The Choice of Reactions

Rich DeVos once asked Scott Brayton, an accomplished racing driver and a friend of his, how he reacted during a race like the Indy 500, when cars started piling up in front of him. "What kind of split-second choices do you have at speeds of more than 200 miles an hour?" Brayton replied that, through long hours of experience in practicing how to make the right moves during *small* collisions, he had learned not to panic or freeze during such momentous crises. As a result, he could calculate almost instantaneously where an opening was going to be so he could steer through the accident zone unscathed.

He had grasped how to program himself in order to make the choice that would literally save his neck. You can readily apply that lesson to your own life. Making the right choice depends upon staying alert. And alertness means first recognizing the existence of a choice, then having a clear head and the experience to know how to select the best alternatives under any circumstance.

But how do you react when it seems apparent that you really do not have any choice—when something is "inevitable"? People constantly reiterate that certain events prove the inevitability of it all. Some of the examples they voice are

- Being laid off from your job
- Having one's house burn to the ground
- Watching a loved one die

Inevitable? Not so.

In rebuttal, Jay Van Andel asserts, "You always have the choice of what attitude to take. And your answer to adversity can, in effect, change the impact that the 'inevitable' has on your life and well-being."

He talks about meeting a young lady who aspired to be a musician and join one of the top symphony orchestras in the Midwest. At the age of eighteen, she was hailed as a budding virtuoso when she exhibited unusual talent as a violinist. Then she lost her left hand in an auto accident. "You could say that her career was doomed, that she had no choice," he said, "that is, until she learned how to live with this traumatic reality. She transferred her talents to the organ and became an exciting performer, a fine teacher of music, and an inspiration for three generations of churchgoers."

There are two other ways to look at the subject of choice.

1. What do you do with *failure?*
2. What do you do with *success?*

The two hardest things in life to deal with are at the opposite ends of the pole: success and failure. Which one would you choose? Well, you do have a choice! And your choice is likely to affect the future as well as the present, since success commonly breeds success and failure tends to beget failure.

If you feel that not many people would actually choose failure over success, you may be surprised at what we have to say about that later on in this book.

SELF STARTER

Before finding out what we are going to reveal, see if you can think of at least one person among your friends or acquaintances who deliberately failed at something in order to succeed in a different way.

The Choice Begins at Home

Look around you. Who are your friends and associates? What do they mean to you, both personally and in your various fields of endeavor? Where would you stand if the people with whom you had chosen to associate were completely different?

The first area of choice to consider is the one that is most immediate: your own family. This may seem paradoxical because there is no way you can select your blood relatives. Like sun and shadow, they are there, playing their role in lighting your course through life. You may not be able to pick your relatives, but you can certainly select those to whom you pay attention and with whom you associate most frequently.

Never married, a maiden lady we'll identify only as Adele was often evaluated by her two sisters as lacking in the important qualities of womanhood while they produced five successful children. But one of her male cousins found her far more interesting than her siblings and encouraged her to develop her creative skills. He was instrumental in helping her become an able marketing director in a large corporation. She overcame her shyness and her "spinster" designation and later married a widower whose three adult children came to adore her and made her godmother to their own children.

Knowing her, we are convinced she would have blossomed much earlier in life had she chosen to associate with the right relatives instead of the nay-saying ones.

Why do so many people see their dreams fade and their aspirations die? Because they choose to listen to the negative opinions of members of their own family. Many people learn how to deal effectively with their enemies, yet ironically they cannot deal with relatives who are naysayers and pessimists, constantly pricking the balloons of hope.

SELF STARTER

List four relatives who fit the positive and negative roles. What can you learn from—or about—each of these people and your power of choice?

How many times have you expressed a personal enthusiasm about a better job, an improved lifestyle, an unusual venture, only to have someone close to you point out all the pitfalls that will surely make your dream impossible to attain? All too often, it is the easiest thing in the world to find some relative who will tell you what you cannot accomplish, and why.

Your choice of associations with members of your family must be developed as a system of checks and balances. You have to make a firm decision to close your ears to certain persons, just as you have to emphasize your belief in your own worth.

Coping with the Wrong Choices

Not uncommon in family life is the case of the person who arises in the morning ready to tackle some challenge. All at once some member of the household who has gotten up on the wrong side of bed informs him that he looks tired and pale and the skies are threatening rain. In no time at all, he really does feel a bit run down and the idea of going forth into clammy dampness begins to loom as an unpleasant chore. All the spark goes out of his earlier enthusiasm.

If you are faced with this kind of situation, and it gets to the point where it can seriously affect your attitude and your work, your best course of action is to avoid that particular family member whenever you are about to embark on an important enterprise. You really do have the power of choice, even in a skittish circumstance like this. Never relinquish that power of choice out of a misguided sense of loyalty to a blood relative.

How to Choose the Bright Side

The opposite alternative is far more productive. You get up in the morning feeling tired and listless and your children tell you how great you look and what a fine day it is for whatever you have planned. In the wink of an eye, you've decided that you were wrong and your family is right. Result: You quickly regain your bounce and are ready for whatever the morning may bring.

The vitality of the American system of government depends not so much on the pomp and circumstance of the House and Senate as it does on what goes on in each individual home. The family heads the list of institutions crucial to the American way of life. And the atmosphere of the home is crucial in shaping the kinds of decisions and choices people make in their daily lives over periods of years and generations.

An increasingly complex family culture has threatened and placed great stress on intimate personal relationships today. Among the changes in the last two generations, for example, are these:

- Increase in the number of two-income homes
- Dispersal of family members to more and more distant locations
- Increase in mixed marriages and more frequent associations with other ethnic groups
- Increase in divorces and single-parent situations

Despite the continuing evolutions, the family is the place to start if you want to choose a more positive and productive life. The determination of priorities within the family is a process that utilizes familiar, everyday situations. That process can condition people to face the more complex problems of life on all fronts. If you can help to train members of your own family to make positive choices, you will be doing them and yourself an enduring and valuable service. Members of even the poorest families have a priceless contribution that can be donated at no cost: the gift of encouragement. Never be afraid to encourage those you love to reach for the stars. The road to success is paved with the building blocks of people who refused to give up, who persisted, finally overcame their problems, and reached their goals. Failure itself can often motivate success.

The man who was without doubt the most prolific inventor in American history, Thomas Edison, persevered through so many failed attempts, wrote one of his biographers, that sometimes he was perceived as having arrived at his solutions by sheer accident. "In trying to perfect a thing," wrote Edison, "I sometimes run up against a granite wall a hundred feet high. If, after trying and trying and trying again, I can't get over it, I turn to something else. Then some day—it may be months or it may be years later—something is discovered which I recognize may help me scale at least part of that wall."

Caring and Sharing—Priceless Family Assets

There are two types of families all of us know well. The first, which we do our best to avoid, is the family whose members are constantly bickering and finding fault with each other, all the while compounding individual miseries in a kind of group discontent.

SELF STARTER

Picture a family you know that fits this category and list five of its most irritating qualities or typical actions.

Conversely, there is the family whose solidarity is assured because the members care deeply for each other and are supportive, no matter how many troubles they face individually and collectively. These people not only care, they share. They give instant and heartfelt recognition to one another's accomplishments rather than jealously downgrading the value of achievements. And they choose to help carry the burdens of any family member who is discouraged or down on his luck, sharing their own good fortune with the others so that all can benefit.

SELF STARTER

Now picture a family you know that fits this category and list five of its characteristics that you would most like to see emulated in other families.

If you can help your own parents, children, siblings, and peers understand the value of these positive interactive attitudes and reflect the same outlook, you will have forged a strong link in the chain of success, happiness, and fulfillment.

A responsibility of parents is to mold loving, lasting relationships with their children. Parental guidance simply cannot be delegated. Strong families are molded by people of conviction who believe enough in the value of parenthood to pattern their entire lives, if necessary, around home and family. That is not to say that parents must sacrifice their careers, personal goals, or the quality of their performance in other areas of life, but they must make some considered choices.

Looking at the other side of the coin, children (of all ages) have a responsibility to cooperate in mutual efforts to encourage family relationships in ways that are positive and supportive. However, they must also be able to broaden their associations with those outside the family so that they can better evaluate the quality of the family influences that are shaping their lives. They do themselves a disservice if they automatically equate age with wisdom or embrace all the values held by their parents.

One unfortunate choice that too many parents make, for example, is to focus on money as a goal and to foster dismal comparisons with other families who have "made it" financially. Money may be essential for the attainment of certain goals, but it should never be the goal itself. We all know the clichés: "Money can't buy happiness," and "The best things in life are free." There is a great deal of truth in those old lines. Native health, sunshine, fresh air, the beauties of nature, and innate abilities *are* free. All things being equal, though, you can enhance your life and lifestyle by enjoying many of the things that are not free, too, as long as you keep your values in proper balance.

President Jimmy Carter is a fine example of a man who has few financial needs and could sit back and contemplate the world at his leisure without lifting a finger. Yet he has carved a whole new career for himself—to his great credit and despite what his detractors might have thought about him as president—by guiding a program that is bringing comfort to thousands of people in need. Working tirelessly for Habitat for Humanity, he has been instrumental in doing something about the plight of desperately poor families who need suitable low-cost housing. Explaining why he and his wife have given many hours of their own time to this program, he says, "We see Habitat as one of today's greatest 'investments' in the compassion available to people who want to help others."

This former president could easily have made a choice no one would have quarreled with and elected to undertake some of the usual pursuits available to retired people of means.

Turning Negative Choices into Positive Action

Newspapers and TV news programs today are replete with the pathetic stories of disintegrating families whose individual members are constantly fighting each other or denying their roots. Typically, young people in these family situations go out into the streets on their own at far too early an age and almost inevitably are swallowed up by a hostile environment. When you take kids and throw them into a mob where they are scared for their lives, pretty soon they become part of the mob, just to survive. You don't have to look far in daily newspapers to read alarming accounts of teenagers arming themselves with knives and guns to protect themselves from peers who are similarly fortified. These deeply disturbing negative choices—as well as others less extreme—have resulted in the failures of generations of young people.

SELF STARTER

Clip some typical examples from your local paper. Are any of these alarmingly close to examples you know about personally? List a few such situations.

Today we are living with third-generation welfare kids, because they and their parents and grandparents were in dismal situations where they elected to choose welfare as a way of life. The children grew up with a philosophy of welfare, they chose to accept it, and their children in turn accept it, thinking it is their inherited, inalienable right. The only ones who change and break the pattern in this kind of family situation are the fortunate few who yank themselves loose from those hostile environments and make the decision to become associated with people whose concepts and lifestyles are markedly different.

We knew one young man who exemplified the last-mentioned case and who was able to break the chain. After several brushes with the law, when he narrowly avoided a jail sentence, he was placed on probation and ordered to perform 100 hours of public service. Since he was athletic, he elected to assist with a softball program for handicapped boys. He became so involved in the determination of these young patients to break through the handicap barrier and lead normal lives that he continued working in the program long after his probation had ended. Within a year, he himself had enrolled in a health orientation program and eventually became a physical education teacher.

We don't mean to push the environmental factor beyond reason. Inheritance does play a part, as we see in the case of some adoptive parents who find that the children they have taken into their family are of a strikingly different mold from their own, despite love and attention and a seeming adjustment to a new environment. People who come from one set of parents cannot be expected to graft automatically onto new roots. However, they can be guided to a remarkable extent by people who are themselves achievers and who can motivate them to try to choose positive objectives that are within their capabilities.

"There are many rewards for those who open their homes— and their hearts—to young people in need of a family," says Rich DeVos. "We see this procedure as an admirable example of turning a negative into a positive. Adults, however, whether dealing with children who are their own flesh and blood or with ones who are adopted, must encourage them to associate with people whose friendship will be affirmative and meaningful. Once young people have chosen to attach themselves to certain types of people, it is not always easy to break away and become associated with different groups. We have seen this with our own children and with the children of our friends. Parents can only go so far in trying to motivate their offspring to seek out the kinds of friends who will be compatible and beneficial in the long run. But they have to make the attempt and express real personal interest, or else risk suffering the consequences."

Marriage is a good case in point. Is the spouse you select going to be supportive and inspire you to get more out of life and accomplish your goals? Or will the marriage simply set up unwanted obstacles and restrictions?

SELF STARTER
How supportive are you? What could you do to be more understanding? What desirable results might ensue?

Many people back away from trying to influence their children in the matter of marriage. "If you tell your son a certain girl is no good for him," goes the argument, "then he'll react in just the opposite way and be determined to marry her. But if you withhold your personal opinions, he'll probably find out for himself in time to break off the engagement."

"In our experience," adds Jay Van Andel, "the best choice is to risk being perfectly honest about communicating your doubts and your reasons behind them. If you have been communicating right along on other subjects of family concern and dealing with your sons and daughters openly and honestly, then you stand a better chance of being listened to with an open mind when you express opinions about love and marriage.''

Of Critics and Criticism

There is an old Swedish axiom that advises, ''You should choose your associates while it is still daylight.''

You would do well to go one step farther and make the selection only on bright days when the sun is full on the face of everyone present. There are simply too many people out there who *seem* to be the kinds of achievers we would like to see, but who turn out to be masters at putting people down. We live in an age when not a few of our ''heroes'' seem to be people who are rabid critics and detractors. Audiences listening to commentators on the podium actually cheer when the speakers tear people and systems to shreds. The ''roast'' as a form of social entertainment is popular today—yet often on a damaging and demeaning level.

If we spend too much of our time finding fault, however amusing, we will never have the incentive to accentuate the positive. Critics have their rightful place in society, but not when they deliberately pull a ''rip-job'' just for the effect. It is much easier to unmask flaws than to produce goods and good works. We get tired of the way many so-called ''whistle-blowers'' and ''watchdogs'' constantly talk the economy down, with no real respect for the miracles of technology and manufacturing that have made autos, computers, appliances, and other remarkable inventions possible.

Based on long experience in dealing with people of all ages and types and from every imaginable background, Van Andel and DeVos have

a real preference for those who inspire rather than conspire. We explicitly choose to deal with persons who can accept life for what it is, rather than with those 'brilliant' types who can spout their heady interpretations of what is wrong with the state of the economy, the government, and the world.

We do not mean to imply that all criticism is an evil. We are human enough so that when someone informs us we have done something 'wrong,' it is only natural to react by taking offense and trying to counterattack. Yet it is important to recognize the fact that some criticism can be positive and productive. People who react constructively to criticism first evaluate the source of it. They pay little attention to the naysayers who make a hobby of panning institutions and putting people down. But they listen carefully if the criticism comes from a source that is both objective and trustworthy.

In so doing, they try to moderate their natural feelings of indignation and seek to understand their critics. At the very least, this approach sometimes leads a critic to modify a comment that was too harsh or to explain the meaning behind a statement that may have sounded more negative than was intended.

SELF STARTER

Can you find an example of this in your own community? What happened? And how did this markedly change the outcome?

What it all boils down to in the end is that we have to live together with other people, and will never all see eye to eye. Individuals can, of course, choose to live alone in the wilderness. They can also remain among other people but choose to be uncommunicative and loners. Or they can recognize that humans really are gregarious by nature and that their choice is to be part of the larger community, accepting the fact that healthy give and take are all part of living together.

Many years ago, in the roughest and poorest area of Montgomery, Alabama, a sharecropper's daughter, Consuello Harper, stood in the rain outside a grungy pool hall telling the pimps, prostitutes, and winos they could be somebody if they would only choose to try. They weren't buying her lecture. They heaped abusive language on her and one drunk spit in her face. Now, more than two decades later, "Connie" Harper is still delivering her message of self-help. But the pool hall has been replaced by a well-constructed training center that has guided more than 6,000 people to infinitely better ways of life. Having taken her share of verbal, mental, and even physical abuse, this indominitable lady has proven her critics wrong and turned her detractors into admirers. "No more welfare," she insists. "You have to give people a hand up, not a handout."

It is all too easy these days to fall into the company of the naysayers because they sound so logical and have become so well accepted by society. Thus, it is even more vital to link yourself with friends and associates who perceive this trend toward negativism and give it the brush-off it merits. When, for example, you set yourself up in a partnership or a team, the outcome will depend a great deal on the person or persons you include in this "link." Do you really want one of the above-mentioned naysayers as an associate—a person who chooses always to look at the negatives that stand in the way of success and fulfillment and will create a barrier to personal achievement? "Looking back on our own careers," says DeVos, "we hate to think what would have happened if we had chosen to become associated with the wrong people or if we, as partners, had not shared the same kinds of commitments and goals."

When it comes to a matter of choice, Epictetus, a canny philosopher of the fifth century, stated the matter about as simply and believably as anyone ever will: "Everything has two handles, by one of which it ought to be carried and by the other not."

CHAPTER
2

Choosing to Get Motivated

"In any sense in which we can choose what action we shall do, we can choose what *motive* we shall act from."

—Charles S. Peirce

You can choose to do something you honestly believe in. Yet belief is just half the answer. Posted above the doorway to the football locker room at the University of Michigan is a sign that is a constant reminder to players that determination can lead to excellence: "What the mind can conceive and believe, the mind can achieve."

Can people really achieve anything they choose to put their minds to? Positive thinking has acquired a bad name in some quarters because a few people claim too much for it. We are sometimes asked to believe that if you think positively long enough and hard enough, you can shed pounds, acquire the skills of a professional athlete, or build a profitable and successful business.

Thinking positively and believing in your abilities, however, must function within sensible bounds. First, your belief must be based on facts. A politician, for example, can claim to be as eloquent as Abe Lincoln, but without developing the insight, talents, and compassion of a true statesman, he will still sound as boring as yesterday's news.

Second, belief must be backed by action. Take the case of the high school janitor who performed his job well in spite of the fact that he could neither read nor write. When the school board established minimum literacy standards for all employees, the janitor was fired. Undaunted, he went on to establish his own janitorial service, which became so successful that he was soon earning more than the people who fired him.

While discussing his business with his banker one day, the

banker remarked, "Imagine what you could have done if you had been able to read and write."

"If I could read and write," came the reply, "I'd still be a high school janitor!"

The point here, of course, is that belief in oneself, backed by a firm commitment to achieve a chosen goal, will ultimately lead to success. Neither faith nor action *alone* will accomplish that. To believe in a foolish notion—even sincerely and completely—still adds up to foolishness. In a like manner, action without purpose is just wasted motion. Only when you forge unshakable faith with unbreakable will can you count on unlimited success.

The Value of Choosing Winners

When the janitor was dumped, he decided that this act simply was not going to make him a loser in life. Instead of fretting and making excuses, he went on to a much better career. The act of "dumping" is a two-edged sword. Never feel guilty about avoiding—even dumping—people whom you once hoped to encourage as friends but who have become negative in their outlooks and are slowly dragging you down to their level. It may seem harsh or unsympathetic to advise such a step, but as long as you choose to hang around with dead-end people, you're going to be a dead-ender yourself. If you associate with losers, you'll become a loser. Conversely, if you choose to associate with winners, you will become a winner.

SELF STARTER

Since it helps to have an image in mind, picture two people you know who are winners and two who are losers. Ask yourself what situations might result if you were associated in any kind of venture with each of these people.

No matter how strongly motivated you may be, and no matter how convinced you are that you can change the world and remold people in your own image, don't risk it. Few of us are rugged enough or gifted enough to swim against the tide. Try as you might, you can seldom overcome the opposing forces that will hold you back relentlessly. The fact is, people often use this form of negativism to prevent other people from outclassing them in life.

Ridicule, sarcasm, and scorn are the powerful tools of people with negative attitudes about their lives and their work. "Who do you think you are?" they say, when you propose an idea that is unfamiliar to them and beyond the usual goals. "What makes you think you can do it?" "Let's not make laughingstocks out of ourselves."

You may start off resisting the skeptics with unabashed confidence, but if you listen long enough to all the reasons why you cannot succeed in a certain venture or plan of action, you'll end up believing the outspoken critics rather than your own judgment.

People with problems of insecurity or doubt or lack of motivation go to psychiatrists for years to get themselves shored up. Yet still they fail to change because, in most cases, they continue to exist in the same negative environment of their choice, surrounded by people who are everlastingly reminding them of their flaws and weaknesses.

You can easily be misled, quite innocently, by hanging around with the wrong crowd because of some common hobby or interest that seems to make you mutually compatible. You see this happening to kids all over the country. They cling to a motorcycle gang because, as it turns out, they just happen to like motorcycles. Or they spend most of their time at video arcades playing electronic games, or following the mob to rock concerts. Soon, they are led by the ringleaders of the groups into bad habits—sampling drugs, breaking minor laws, and then phasing into more and more serious problems—without being aware that an insidious transformation has been taking place.

SELF STARTER

List a few situations familiar to you that fit this category, and that perhaps have impacted on your own life and objectives.

One of the great tragedies of today's society is the number of young people who are destroying the finest tool they have— their minds—by taking drugs. Why do young people get hooked on drugs? There are no pat answers for a problem that is so complex. But one common reason is certainly fear: the fear of failure, or not being accepted by their peers, or facing real and imagined threats. And so they turn to substance abuse. They have made a crucial, self-defeating choice, yet without ever realizing that sad fact of life until it was too late.

We are all familiar with examples of celebrities who recount horror stories about appalling circumstances in which they found themselves and which were ruining their lives. In the fortuitous cases, they realized the problems in time to effect a turnabout. But the less fortunate ended up having to face personal disasters over which they no longer could exert any control. Among the more familiar examples was that of the basketball star, "Magic" Johnson, and his battle with AIDS. It is one of those cases that people describe with the preface, "If only. . . "

When young people are in high school, they are pretty much thrown together and have a difficult time associating or disassociating on their own. Once they get to college or into the workforce, however, they can make decisions about the people with whom they will circulate and live. Many make the mistake of feeling sorry for certain people they have met. Convinced that there is strength in numbers, they believe that eventually they will straighten one another out. Sympathy is a fine virtue, but *misplaced* sympathy can be ruinous.

In making this kind of choice, those young people tumble into a very common pitfall. They have come to realize that successful people can teach failed people or people who might otherwise be failures. But what they do not yet understand is that failed people or people who have yet to attain their own level of success can seldom teach others how to be achievers.

> **SELF STARTER**
> Think of typical situations in which you can relate
> levels of success. Do you play tennis, golf, hand-
> ball, or some other competitive sport? If so, you
> probably prefer to play with people who are slightly
> better than you are and who will thus upgrade your
> level of play, rather than pulling you down a rung
> or two.

Look for people who are going in the same direction you
have chosen and who are on at least the same achievement
plane and preferably a little bit higher. Continuously evaluate
the standings of your friends and associates. If they are the
kind who prefer to bum around street corners, watch TV aim-
lessly, and read trashy books and magazines, then it is difficult
for you to aim higher without exposing yourself to their ridicule or displeasure. If, on the other hand, you have selected
the kinds of friends who enjoy the arts and good literature
regularly, and who use their time productively, you are likely
to do the same or risk being expelled from their ranks.

The process is really very simple. You have to play the part,
and the more vigorously the better. Arthur J. Forrest, who started
his career as an orphan, with no money and a tenth-grade education, was advised to accept a routine, low-paying position. He refused, managed to borrow a small sum, and went into business
for himself. Years later, having founded a very successful manufacturing company, and having contributed regularly to educational institutions, he said in a speech to high-school seniors,
"Success is yours for the *acting*. A man is never a failure until he
acts like one. He may be low on finances, but he is never broke as
long as his process of mind produces thought that can be sold at a
profit. If he desires health, happiness, and prosperity, he must
claim them, for they are his birthright. He must claim them
through positive thought and action."

"I Can Do It!"—The Most Challenging Choice

It is not enough to have the education, brightness, and innate
capability to achieve something; you must also have the desire

and that desire must be motivated and constructive.

Be wary, though, of people who claim that they are motivated and want to get ahead but who constantly are changing jobs. First they are selling products, then they are in real estate, and after that they decide they should open up a shop or get a job in an office, or try their hand at some kind of craft. They never stick with any job long enough to make it a career.

By contrast, an excellent way to improve your own productivity is to be with people who know how to use time effectively. These are the individuals who say in a positive, self-assured manner, "I *can* do it!" no matter how "impossible" their objective may seem to the scoffers and detractors.

SELF STARTER

Make a list of people you know in the following categories, to provide a clearer image of the types we have mentioned above: (a) a "king of the hill" pusher, (b) a "rotator" who never stays with the same job, and (c) an achiever who constantly reiterates, "I can do it!"

The rewards of making the right choices, at the right time and in the right place, can make all the difference in your life, in your lifestyle, and in your relationships with others. Once you have made choices about those relationships and then determined how to strengthen your associations in a positive way, it is vital for you to believe in yourself and your unlimited potential. If your aim is low, you'll hit what you shoot at: *nothing.* One of the most powerful forces in the world is the will of people who believe wholly in themselves and dare to aim high, not just once but again and again.

As Henry David Thoreau wrote, "In the long run, men hit only what they aim at. Therefore, though they should fail immediately, they should aim at something high."

Rich DeVos emphasizes again and again that "*I can!*" is the shortest, most powerful sentence you can use. For most people, that assertion works wonders. You can do what you believe you can do. The gap between what you aspire to achieve and what you actually can achieve is very narrow. But first, you must believe.

The nature of your goal makes little difference. No aspects of your life are more important than the combination of faith in self and personal efforts to justify that faith. You name it—your career, business, athletics, the arts, education, church work, politics, marriage—every facet of your life can be guided by this common denominator.

You won't know what you can accomplish until you try. This truth is so simple that people tend to overlook it. You can worry about a problem forever and never solve it—unless you try.

Give things a chance to happen. No life is more tragic than that of the person who nurses a dream or ambition, always wishing but never really choosing to take the right course of action, to give the dream a chance to come true. Some people are so afraid of failure that they inevitably fail.

If you expect something bad to happen, you will almost always be right. In reverse, if you expect good things to occur, events will usually justify your optimism. Underline the positive passages and look upward! As the words of a popular tune had it some years ago, ''Accentuate the positive.''

What many people do not realize is that they can be optimists even though at the same time they realize that sorrows exist and life is not all roses. An upward look is not a luxury; it's a necessity for people who want to be happy and productive.

There are plenty of events to cause us to look downward—the state of the economy, the high crime rate, the rising prevalence of drugs, and increasing taxes, to name just a few. However, it is one thing to recognize the problems and adjust to them and quite another to dwell on them constantly in a negative way.

We live in an exciting world, crammed with far more opportunities than our grandparents and forebears ever could have imagined. And we live in a land where the choices are broader and more dramatic than anywhere else on earth. Great events lie around every corner. It is time that we recognize the marvels and improvements that have influenced our lives.

It is time, too, that we look to the positive things in life and minimize the negative ones.

P/P: The Power of Persistence

Believe not only in yourself but learn how to link your life to those qualities that can strengthen your character and enhance your lifestyle. Among the most vital of these is the *power of persistence.* ''Based on our own experiences,'' says Jay Van Andel, ''if we had to choose the one personal characteristic most associated with success it would be persistence—a strong determination and the will to endure to the end.''

SELF STARTER

Think back in your own experience and list one example of a time when persistence paid off for you, and one when you should have persisted, but did not.

Don't make the mistake some people do of confusing persistence with stubbornness, which exists for its own sake. Persistence has been aptly defined as ''stubbornness with a purpose.''

Support your motivation so consistently with this quality of persistence that you don't have time to listen to all the reasons why you cannot achieve your goals. ''Our fondest wish for individuals bent on success,'' says Jay, ''is not that they bring to the task a massive intellect or well-coordinated body or glib tongue or personal magnetism, but the ability and the will to persist toward their goals.''

Discipline, Discipline, Discipline—A Strong Ally

Motivation is well served, too, by the characteristics of *discipline.* A great Greek scholar advised his pupils some two thousand years ago: ''First, say to yourself what you would be, and then do what you have to do.'' When your motivation and your goals mesh harmoniously, you are far more likely to achieve what you are hoping for than if you have no definite plan of action.

Goal-setting is a vital part of the process of making choices, necessitating discipline to keep you on track and on time. Every day you wait, you lose. You will never achieve your goals if you spend your time thinking and planning, and waiting. This kind of indecision is very common, and it is the wrong way to try to become a success. You might be surprised at what can be accomplished when you say to yourself, "I'm going to make my decision and do that now—not wait for tomorrow in the hope that the time will be riper!"

"Motivation" is a dynamic tool, not some magical formula or shortcut to success. It combines the realization that you must do the things you know you should do and the realistic appraisal of those talents and skills that can be most favorably applied on your behalf. One reason why sound motivation is so effective is that success is 99 percent a matter of attitude.

No matter how disciplined you are, though, you must be comfortable with the way you look at yourself. It is far too easy to settle for a low—or at least overly modest—opinion of yourself because that way you do not have to make any uncomfortable choices, take the extra effort, or risk failure by trying to make changes. You stay where you are, sedentary and never allowing your inner self to become a part of the person others see on the surface.

You hit what you aim at. Michael Levy, publisher of *Texas Monthly,* once remarked that the biggest reason why more people don't try to take risks is that they can't leap over the hurdle of thinking, "God, I might fail."

We know people for whom that hurdle looms just as high as their self-esteem is low. Weighed down by doubt and indecision, they never generate the self-confidence that would lift them up and over the fear of failure. These are the kinds of people whom President Franklin D. Roosevelt had in mind when he uttered his famous truism, "The only fear we have is fear itself."

Some fears, of course, are not entirely groundless. People who are wrestling with the choice of getting a job with a large company or going into a venture on their own are wise to consider the annual data on small business failures. So why do so many would-be entrepreneurs—more than 600,000 of them in an average year—embark on this shaky road? Some economists say that people just don't believe the statistics, think of them as being rigged, and jump into the fray anyway. But a much more basic and positive motivation for choosing to take the risk, we believe, is the persistent desire of these individuals to exercise their talents, accomplish more, and upgrade their lifestyles.

One of the most vital aspects of self-discipline is the matter of personal time management. People frequently complain loudly that they "don't have time" to do what they need to do in order to succeed. Well, get up an hour earlier and you can add 7 hours to your week, 30 hours to your month, and 360 hours to your year—or more than two weeks annually. "But I can't get up," they say, "I'm still tired." Fine—then go to bed an hour earlier instead of watching television. There is always plenty of time for achievement, if you discipline yourself. But you do have to make the choices. Cut out the periods of inactivity and waste; take less time for lunch; get over the sloppy habits that waste time.

SELF STARTER

Make a list of what you need to do to accomplish your current goals. Writing them down helps to keep your objectives in focus.

Educational Objectives

The successful family is one in which learning—and by that we mean not necessarily school learning, but keeping an open mind and continuing to pursue knowledge and experience—is considered to be a lifelong pursuit. The natural inclination of people to improve their circumstances is the most powerful engine in our society and one that is attained largely through the learning process. Sound judgment and the ability to meet challenges come from discipline and the input of meaningful information daily.

If you can tap a pipeline to knowledge, you can be assured of linking yourself to one of the most potent and motivating forces on earth. Knowledge stimulates belief, and the power of belief is a phenomenon known to man since earliest times. If you know and believe in something with all that is within you, then you can work miracles.

Fear of rejection slays the spirit with a fusillade of what-ifs. But we like a very simple little poem that counters this negative approach:

> Ten times ten I tried and failed,
>   My courage paled.
> Ten times ten plus one I strained,
>   That's when I gained.
> Ten times ten plus two are done,
>   And I have won.

Believe!*

What do you do to get people to choose richer, more meaningful lives? How do you pry them out of their shells? How do you get them to enjoy their present jobs or to be better at them or to be happier in what they are doing?

The answer is found in the most valuable gift you can give a person: encouragement to believe. Too many people say "can't." They can't sell. They can't speak in public. They haven't had the right training or education to tackle some venture. When people are convinced that they cannot do something, then no matter how much you teach them or provide the details and counsel for achievement, they refuse to try. They have already said to themselves, "Well, I can't do that." And that includes trying to make choices in life.

If people are not motivated or are skeptical, then they underestimate themselves and all the details of a job become problems. They cannot undertake certain jobs or accomplish things because they have never done them before and never had any successes to give them confidence. But if people have faith, believe in what they are doing, and are motivated, then they will figure out the details.

*This is the subject of a book and numerous articles by Rich DeVos.

Victim or Victor?

There are two types of individuals: those who believe that they are victims of circumstances and those who believe they control circumstances. The controllers, the ones who have faith and who believe in themselves, make things happen. The key is to do it now. It is often interesting to see what happens when people choose to make things happen. Too many people operate in an atmosphere of thinking that they are being put upon by others, so they do nothing. These people are always waiting for the right time for something to happen.

Many men and women have been reared in an atmosphere that encourages people to wait for the right circumstances. But people who succeed do not wait for something to happen—they make it happen! When you choose to make something happen, you change the circumstances. You decide what to do. It does not matter which side of the bed you actually got up on or how you happened to feel when you woke up. Conditions are never perfect for getting on with something. People say they are too young or too old or too something else. If you don't choose to get around to doing something, it's because you have not yet learned the discipline of controlling the circumstances.

Motivation provides the energy and faith serves as the compass for people who want to strive for excellence, not necessarily at an unrealistic and elevated level, but within the comfortable confines of their own competency and personal goals. People who consolidate their faith will always be the better for it.

SELF STARTER

Jot down the names of two people you know who consider themselves victors and two who moan that they are "victims" of society. How has their attitude affected them in their personal lives and careers?

Attitudes—A Natural Resource

Few people will argue with the assertion that positive attitudes are vital ingredients for young people starting out in careers of their choice. But there should be no cut-off point. Throughout life, you need a positive, hopeful outlook in order to cope and to be effective. Self-doubt leads to disappointment and defeat. Make an inventory of your accomplishments and deficiencies, pinpoint the areas that you need to perfect, and then concentrate on ways to improve and build yourself up.

The best attitude is one that we have come to refer to as the "upward look." This is not to be confused with the superficial perspective of people who like to keep their heads in the clouds and avoid seeing the seamier sides of life. Rather, it is that special talent that makes it possible to find solutions to problems by looking beyond, to the practical ways of solving them.

America has traditionally been a nation that fostered positive attitudes. Can you imagine where we would be today if it had been otherwise? Who would ever have chosen to venture out West with all the dangers and unknown circumstances that the early pioneers faced? Who would have had the temerity to form a new nation and take on the gargantuan problems of our government? Who would have wanted to found fledgling companies and industries or labor from dawn to dusk to grow crops? Or speak out against oppression in the face of vengeful enemies?

Fortunately, today we can be more secure in making such choices, no matter how controversial, because we can look back on the documented records of others who have done so. We can, in effect, have the courage of our convictions.

Evaluating Motivation

Attitudes—no matter how positive or how clear-cut—would be ineffective without the driving force that puts them to work: motivation.

Motivation starts with a hunger, a need. The desire for more money is not a bad motivation, but it is only a symbol for other motivational forces, such as the desire to improve one's lifestyle or living standards, environment, or education. Security is another motivating goal, so is independence, along with certain ego satisfactions. A sense of recognized personal accomplishment can be very satisfying for some people, even more so than money or material things. This is especially true when the motivation leads to voluntary public service, where the financial rewards are nonexistent or very modest.

The desire for education motivates many people, although education itself has been unduly censured by some, including those in leadership positions who have tossed off inflated opinions without thinking them through. Those who pan our educational system and complain about kids not learning "the way our parents and grandparents did" tend to lose sight of the accumulated accomplishments over the decades. Today, for instance, 25 percent of our population is studying in some recognized learning institution, having available the widest variety of curricula ever offered in the nation's history. Moreover, thousands of skilled teachers, facing just the same economic challenges, choices, and problems as any other citizen, are sacrificing larger incomes from better-paying jobs in order to teach our youths—and adults—and are performing a superb service. Not only that, but they are enjoying the benefit of a strengthened education themselves, for, as the old adage has it "to teach is to learn twice over." We should take pride in our American educational system, not debase it.

Why and How Motivation Thrives

There is a certain type of motivation that might be called "reverse motivation," best illustrated perhaps by the rags-to-riches stories of people who were determined to escape the slums in which they spent their childhood. Rich and Jay have always looked at motivation as a positive force, one that helps to make you believe in yourself and head for a target rather than escape from pain and distress.

Most importantly, they insist, you must believe in yourself. You can create an atmosphere of confidence in two ways: by surrounding yourself with positive input and by removing yourself from negative thoughts. Develop an awareness of attitudes of those people with whom you are in constant contact. Avoid the ones who are always carping about the faults of others, who are professional complainers. Ignore the assertions of such critics that people in business tend to be cutthroat and self-serving.

If you want to succeed in a career, in business, in society, in life itself, you can do no better than to tap the many sources of inspiration that can help you lift yourself by your own bootstraps from mediocrity to excellence. Motivate yourself by thinking about the kinds of leaders Thomas Jefferson referred to when he described them as ones "who not only lead but who teach others how to lead."

Motivation is a force that is flexible, not rigid. We have always found it most effective when we have added new challenges, ones that provided some kind of additional inspiration for us and that perhaps led us in the direction of achievements we once thought were unattainable. Always look forward, not back. "A famous golf pro told us," says Rich, "that a golfer who looks back at his last bad shot is just going to hit another bad shot. Never dwell on what went wrong, but only on what you are doing that is right."

Motivation is closely linked to inspiration, which flows from common resources all around us. It is not always easy to read, see, or hear about something that will inspire us. We are so bombarded with information from all sides that trying to make effective choices becomes a greater problem than ever before in the rich history of communication. The media keep proliferating. In addition to the few basic forms that brought messages to our parents and grandparents, we now have television, audio cassettes, videotapes, message recorders, communications satellites, dozens of new types of phone devices, and endless ways of speeding up dialogues almost to the point of frenzy—not to mention the seemingly limitless abilities of the computer to add to the input and output.

Effective inspiration can come only when we discipline ourselves to tune in the positive dialogues and tune out the negative ones. The choices are made somewhat easier in light of the fact that there are probably only one-tenth as many media messages on the positive side as there are on the negative.

Thus, you can weed out a great mass of garbage before you even start the selection process. Even so, people are just not responding as productively as might be expected.

Reading is an important control point because it is personal and can be done at your own pace, in an environment that encourages reflection and a more considered evaluation of facts and opinions. Very few people can cope with television as a means of orderly communication—not when so many, many messages are being thrust at them in rapid-fire and often in helter-skelter fashion. You would be well advised to read books and articles that are positive in outlook, not to see life through rose-tinted glasses but to avoid the avalanche of commentaries that tear society apart just for the sake of being critical or revolutionary.

SELF STARTER

List four books or major articles you have read lately in order of their importance to you. Which were positive in their presentation, and which negative?

We must be inspired by whatever media we select, in such a way that we are perceptive to change and the need for making productive choices so that we can be out front leading the pack and not being dragged behind it. One of the saddest realizations for any leader in the business and industrial world is to see the statistics about the number of companies, large and small, that go bankrupt, have to sell out, or cease operations. What happens in most cases is that these companies are forced out of business because their managers failed to realize the changes taking place in time to make corrective choices of action.

Inspiration/Motivation

What is the relationship between inspiration and motivation?

We are inclined to think, romantically and emotionally, of

inspiration as something that moves us when we hear good music, read a poem or story that touches our heart, or are suddenly struck with an idea that appeals to our sense of creativity. These can be factors, of course, in motivating people to take—or decide to take—some kind of action. But in the overall interpretation of how we are motivated to achieve goals, live better lifestyles, and fulfill our dreams, inspiration is a much more dynamic force. It propels us into the kind of action that will make our lives more meaningful, establish sound relationships with others, and bring rewards, whether in the form of material gains or recognition for accomplishments.

As business leaders, Van Andel and DeVos point out that

We have talked to many people—hundreds, perhaps even thousands—who say in effect, "But I'm just an ordinary kind of person, an average citizen. What is so special about me that suggests any potential for real achievement?"

Our answer to that is: Every individual is unique and special. There is a wealth of good in every person whom God has placed in the world. That good needs only to be discovered, realized, and translated into action through inspiration and motivation.

Inspiration comes in many forms, often surprising ones that we might easily ignore. Consider a story about the noted French artist, Henri Matisse. A visitor to his studio, hoping to discover the secret of his remarkable skill, asked him, "What is the source of your inspiration?"

"Artichokes," came the unexpected answer. "I grow them in my garden. I watch them and see the changing play of light and shade and tone on the leaves and I constantly discover new combinations of colors and patterns. They excite me and they inspire me. Then I go back into the studio and paint."

We all have "artichokes" in our lives, if we can but recognize them and draw inspiration from things that are too often overlooked because they are right there in front of us all along.

CHAPTER
3

Choosing Goals

"Choose always the way that seems the best, however rough it may be; custom will soon render it easy and agreeable."

—Pythagoras

"**T**hirty years ago," reminisces Rich DeVos, who is an accomplished sailor and skipper of racing vessels,

we prepared a short audio cassette that was entitled "Four Winds," which we distributed widely to thousands of people who were associated with us in our business. At the time, we were concerned about a certain weakness we observed in many people who, though working hard and well motivated, seemed to be floundering. Our business was growing substantially and we were expanding steadily into new regions abroad, as well as across the United States and Canada. So there was no reason why anyone in our business should be encountering these difficulties.

What was the problem? Was there a lack of motivation? Were the goals poorly defined?

A little study and evaluation quickly made it clear that this kind of personal disadvantage was by no means confined to our business, but was commonplace in just about every field of endeavor. A large percentage of people simply were failing to establish any goals at all. Thus, no matter how much time they spent or how hard they worked, they lacked direction. The cassette, "Four Winds," referred to the America's Cup Race, which at that time [1958] was won by the yacht, *Columbia,* largely because her crew members knew how to use the winds to their advantage. No matter what direction the wind came from, the skipper was prepared to chart his course so he could take advantage of it. He had a goal, well defined and clear-cut, and he stuck to it.

The trick is to get the boat moving and keep it moving. And you can use this as a simile in almost everything you do. If you know your goal and have faith in it, you won't be thrown off course by adversity. You'll learn how to control the wind instead of letting it control you. People often succeed, not because they have mastered a great challenge in life but because they have learned how to shift a little bit here and there—to "get the right air" as they say in sailing terminology—and they get just enough of an edge on their competitors or adversaries so they come up winners.

It is not always easy to judge the winds, or any other forces of nature. But taking the time and making the effort to do so will pay off. We did some research about people one time and their ability to get things done and we discovered a very interesting fact: weather and climate play a vital part in the accomplishments of man. If you look back in history you will find that the four seasons stimulate action by the very fact that they force change. Those nations that have accomplished the most are the ones located in regions of the earth where there are changing seasons, while those that have year-round summer, as in the Equatorial belts, tend to foster a "mañana syndrome" among their inhabitants—don't do anything today, wait until tomorrow!

We have a regular correspondent, whom we have never met or spoken to on the phone. But we know a great deal about his character and temperament for he is constantly writing us letters. Each one has a new excuse—sometimes quite elaborate and imaginative—explaining why he has not gone to make any calls or sought out any prospective customers. We often wonder how much he might have accomplished had he spent his letter-writing time and ingenuity on business instead of excuses! As the Irish novelist and poet said, "The difficulty in life is the choice."

Establishing Your Priorities

Focus is important. Once you know what your objectives are, establish your priorities. You have to sacrifice certain activities in order to zero in on others that have higher priority. Too many people waste time looking back at what they did wrong instead of ignoring the mistakes and moving forward.

SELF STARTER

List in order three priorities you have—business, social, or otherwise—for next week. Do they come to mind quickly or do you have to struggle to decide what they are?

Benjamin Franklin made sound choices and avoided worrying about difficult decisions and priorities by using what he referred to as his *pro* and *con* device. He divided a sheet of paper into two columns, writing "pro" over one and "con" over the other. Then, over a period of several days, he entered in the appropriate column all the facts he could think of for and against any choice. In the end, he crossed out the entries on one side versus the other that seemed to have equal weight. He also crossed out one weighty factor in one column versus two or three of lesser weight in the facing column. He then reached a decision, based on the number of positive or negative reasons still remaining.

Listening to People Who Counsel Wisely

In selling, for example, the people who dwell on the rejections they've had pretty soon accept themselves as failures. If you undertake to collect money for your church (or any other good cause), accept the fact that some people are going to turn you down. Don't interpret these denials as failures on your part. Go on to the next people on the list. If they give, be thankful. If they don't give, thank them anyway. Don't get hung up on the impression that you are failing or there's something wrong with the program. Your job is to make the calls, not to try to pressure people into giving and then feeling guilty when your efforts are fruitless.

It's tough if you have not developed self-respect, but very easy if you have taken the time to find out who you are and what you can do.

People become obsessed sometimes with reading about so-called "success stories." They seem to feel that success will rub off on them if they learn everything they can about how someone else was successful. But, in all honesty, the only success story that is important is your own. What have you done? Or are doing? Or will do? We don't want to hear all about "this guy in California. . . ." We want to know who *you* are and what you are up to.

When you make a speech, talk about the things that relate to your own career, your life, your experiences, not those of a lot of other people. That way, you'll never need notes and you'll never have to worry whether the details are right. When you relive your own story, you also talk in a more animated and credible fashion. You become convincing.

Keeping Your Eye on the Target

Channel every waking thought to the objectives you have set for yourself. The Bible says, "As a man thinks so is he." What you accomplish depends upon the way your mind functions. What the mind can conceive, man can achieve because the mind is all powerful. If you believe this, you will see it.

When your mind concentrates on a goal, you will achieve it. But if your mind is divided, your goal will be fractured. The key here is single-mindedness. But you must have a goal in mind, a dream. Remember those lyrical lines from the hit musical, *South Pacific:* "If you don't have a dream, how are you going to make your dream come true?"

Woodrow Wilson once said, when asked how people achieved great things and became famous, "We grow great by dreams. All big men are dreamers."

Wilson was a man who knew the power of setting goals. During World War I, acting as commander-in-chief of American forces, he ordered the U.S. Navy to mine the English Channel. "But, Mr. President," protested the top admiral, "I can't possibly lay mines across the whole English Channel!"

"Can you lay *one* mine?" asked Wilson.

"Yes, of course I can," replied the admiral.

"Well, then," said the president, "lay down one mine, then

lay down another, and another until you get the job done.''

The secret to life's goals is to do one at a time, then another and another. Begin today by establishing at least one goal. You'll be delightfully surprised at your progress.

"Inch by inch, anything is a cinch," Van Andel and DeVos like to say, citing their good friend and renowned minister, Robert H. Schuller, who has successfully counseled many people who were failing in life because they were trying to make impossible leaps instead of a sensible daily progression.

By focusing on a goal, you concentrate on things that are positive and avoid one of the most devastating weaknesses in today's society, negative thinking. A companion fault is the "do-nothing" attitude. We all know of hundreds of people in our town who are great *spectators*. But we can count on the fingers of one hand the number who are great competitors. It's easy to sit in the stands or in front of the TV set and cheer your lungs out. But to get out there on the field and sweat and strain and risk discomfort and possible injury—that's for the other guy! Besides, you've been working hard all week and what you really need at this time and place is relaxation, not antagonism.

Adjust your eye level upward.

Taking this kind of optimistic stand and establishing goals makes it easier for you to sell yourself on *you,* and sell *you,* in turn, to others. In a book entitled *How to Be Your Own Best Friend,* two psychologists made the convincing point that they had discovered in their research into human behavior that the real source of happiness and achievement is within us, not outside, and that most people have not even begun to tap their own potential and are operating way below capacity. And they will continue that way as long as they look for someone to give them the keys to the kingdom.

"You have to make the basic decision," they explained. "Do you want to lift yourself up or put yourself down? Many people are literally their own worst enemy."

It is up to each of us to give ourselves some recognition for our achievements. If we wait for it to come from others, we feel resentful when nothing matures. Doing what makes you feel good about yourself is *not* self-indulgence.

Studying a Range of Universal Goals

At the end of the 1950s, President Dwight D. Eisenhower decided that it was time for Americans to evaluate and state their goals, both as individuals and as members of the world's greatest democracy. Accordingly, a commission of noted leaders in the nation was formed and many great people addressed themselves to the question, "What are our goals?"

The answer, published in book form in 1960, was 372 pages long! It is doubtful that many individuals waded through the accumulated dissertations and essays and statements that seemed necessary to interpret that single five-letter word. Looking at the subject from a national viewpoint, the answer was pretty much summed up in two sentences: "The paramount goal of the United States was set long ago. It is to guard the rights of individuals, to ensure their development, and to enlarge their opportunities."

That hits home. What goal could be more precise for you than one that protects your rights, provides opportunities for personal growth, and opens up doors for the future?

The report pinpointed one other factor that we have always considered very important in establishing goals. As it stated, "Often one thinks of a goal as something which can be *attained.* But . . . a goal is necessarily a *moving,* not a fixed target . . . *directions* in which we should move and keep moving, not fixed points which we can attain and then relax."

One of the interesting conclusions reached by this immense study was that, although it stated the goals of Americans collectively as a uniform objective, it pointed out that the goals of individuals had to be as diverse and different as the individuals themselves. "Goals must consist of efforts to encourage and bring to fulfillment the best of what already exists in embryo."

"It has been our experience," says DeVos,

that most people underestimate their capabilities and capacities. You have merely to look at history to realize what individuals *can* do if they set their minds to it. Six of our Presidents, for example, were born in log cabins. Six others were the sons of ordinary farmers and spent their boyhoods working in the fields. Five were sons of artisans and three were born in country parsonages. Never in history have we seen such a record of men rising from humble origins to positions of great influence and responsibility.

If you want further evidence of what can be attained by those who set high goals, sit down and read about the underdogs who have come from nowhere to win medals in the Olympics or other international sporting events.

We like to point to the example of a young lady named Madeline Manning Mims who was voted the World's Greatest Athlete three years in a row by America's sports writers. Yet she had spinal meningitis as a child, a disease that could have kept her crippled beyond hope. With the help of her mother's confidence and prayers, she overcame her disability.

"My condition became a blessing in disguise," she said. "I began to develop a 'never give up' spirit. I learned to be an overcomer."

An "impossible" goal? Suppose it actually had been beyond her reach. She still would have accomplished great strides in overcoming her disability and learning to move forward rather than slump back and indulge in self-pity.

Few people know how to set goals realistically. They set such high goals that they never achieve them but become frustrated in the attempt. Or they set a goal that is so far off that they become discouraged long before they achieve what they intended. A better choice is to establish intermediate objectives that are both logical and attainable. At the same time, every intermediate goal has to be replaced by a new one. Otherwise, when you reach your goal your motivation will cease.

People set goals, then decide they are too ambitious and, with so much emphasis on the "get rich quick" mentality, try shortcuts. There is a temptation in life to try to get motivated without doing anything much. There is always the diet plan where you don't have to give up anything. Or the exercise formula that can condense an hour's exertion into three minutes. The world is filled with false, deceptive ways to achieve something for nothing. The state lottery is a good example of a shortcut that is false, because almost everybody will fail. Keep in mind that old Better Business Bureau warning, "If it sounds too good to be true, it probably is."

When it comes to setting goals, choice is very critical because if you set the wrong goals you can waste a lot of time trying to backtrack. That is one reason why so many people do not have any significant goals at all. Another reason is the fear of failure. If you don't set a goal, you won't fail. Also, in our American unstructured society, the choices are so unlimited that it can be bewildering and people become baffled, especially if they have not been given any sense of direction.

One thing we have learned is that there have to be a lot of small goals along the way in order to get to a large goal. These small goals are, of course, easier to attain than the large goal, but they all add up. So after you attain the first goal, you work on the second and the next, and the next, in succession. This adds up to a series of achievements, which become a large achievement. Again, it's a matter of choices for each step. You don't walk up to an airline counter and say to the agent, "I want a ticket for somewhere." You have to decide where you are going to go. In a small way, people go through the process of setting goals and making choices. You seldom jump in your car without having some kind of goal. So, in effect, you are already conditioned to choosing goals and you can go on to more important goals with only a little more reflection and effort.

Another problem in choosing goals is that people tend to be vague about them. In their mind's eye, they see only a fuzzy image of what it is they want to attain, whether for the short term or the long run. The great British writer, Rudyard Kipling, disciplined himself to be specific by composing a poem which he kept constantly in sight:

I keep six honest serving men—
They taught me all I knew.
Their names are *What* and *Why* and *When*
And *How* and *Where* and *Who*.

"Hindcasting," Turning Hindsight into Foresight

As we evaluate the people who have become successful in contrast with those who have not, we find that the latter have often tripped over one of the most common of all stumbling blocks when they tried to set goals for themselves. On the one hand, they are futilely searching for some kind of crystal ball that will give them a preview of the future. On the other hand, they are constantly afflicted with the self-recrimination, "*If only. . .*"

If only I had taken that job with the ABC Company, which has grown from a tiny firm to a large corporation. I could have gotten in on the ground floor and. . .

If only we had purchased that lovely home in the suburbs when the asking price was one-fifth what it is today. Why, we could have sold the place last year, bought a much bigger house, and still had a bundle in the bank. . .

If only we had invested in Glamor Industries when the stock was selling at 3¼ and no one knew what a sleeper it really was. . .

If only I had listened to that manager's counsel about goals for paving the road to a more secure future. . .

The most common regrets in life are the ones that begin with "If only. . . " and paint a glorious picture of what might have been had one enjoyed the vision of foresight.

A friend of ours recently commented, quite seriously, "If only my wife and I had stuck to our agreed-upon goal to give up our drinking and smoking habits ten years ago, do you know what could have happened? We might have invested in the stock market what we spent on booze and butts and built up enough of a nest egg with that money alone to purchase a $150,000 house!"

Strange though it may seem, we have actually discovered a way—we won't call it a formula—for turning hindsight into foresight. We call it *hindcasting*. It is based on a dynamic and forceful, yet simple and straightforward, series of thoughts and actions that transforms hindsight into foresight by using the past to project the future. You can predict the outcome of many kinds of situations you might face by evaluating choices and alternatives you have before you. In business circles, this is termed *risk management,* adapting concepts that have been used successfully by entrepreneurs and others who pioneer in various fields of endeavor.

You can improve your chances of making the right choices and taking the right risks to improve your economic situation and achieve personal goals by studying recent history and following in the footsteps of those who have already undertaken the basic exploration, defined the route, and paved the road. You accomplish this by putting yourself theoretically in the shoes of:

• People who are winners
• Institutions that are winners
• Methods that are winners
• Concepts and faith that are winners
• Careers and avocations that are winners
• Places that are winners
• And everything else that is positive

Through this kind of relationship, you not only nourish those opportunistic forces that will propel you in the right direction, but you learn ahead of time—not when it becomes too late—what kinds of goals you should be setting in order to achieve what you want out of life. You are taking a backward glance and then projecting your sights into the future.

You learn, very simply, *how to turn hindsight into foresight.* And the best place to start in this lifetime quest is with the person on whom you have to rely to make the many choices in life: *yourself.*

SELF STARTER

Jot down descriptions of two instances in the past when you wished earnestly that, in hindsight, you had been able to employ better foresight.

One goal many people have is to be able to hone their anticipatory skills, to learn from past experience and thus turn hindsight into foresight. How can this be achieved? First of all, you have to possess a good memory, to recall the details of what went wrong and what was right with actions in the past. You not only have to remember what you did—or didn't do—but you must be objective enough to admit that you made mistakes and not try to blame failures on other people, or circumstances. It's amazing how certain people can fall into the same old potholes blindly, again and again. They want to ignore the holes or hope they are no longer there. We consider *history* to be one of the most essential subjects in the entire field of education, formal or otherwise. Only by learning what went on in the past can individuals, groups, or whole nations possibly prepare adequately for the future. That is true on a very personal basis as well as in the broadest terms. Some people can train themselves to learn lessons from history, while other people have to put themselves in a more structured learning environment if they want to distinguish fact from fiction and focus on ways to develop their foresight. But not everyone will choose to do this, since it takes time and effort.

"Salesmanship is a good example of the hindsight/foresight problem," explains Jay Van Andel.

Many professional salespersons are good at the careers they chose because they can keep track of the steps that helped them make sales versus those that failed to produce customers. Thus, they can anticipate how a prospective customer will react to a certain sales pitch or course of action. But we have found that many people who have never had sales experience or who hate to sell are often the most effective. Why? Because they are so personally enthusiastic about a product or service that their devotion and exhilaration infect people they are talking to and the latter literally sell themselves. If you look at the situation in a slightly different way, these salespersons are not selling a product or service. They are *recruiting* the prospective customers to take over the selling assignment.

The Winner's Checklist

Among the points related to "hindcasting," which could help you to minimize risks, make more effective choices, and land in the winner's circle are these:

- Interpreting your intuition, the gut feelings that certain options can be right for you, or wrong
- Cultivating patience, a successful way to reduce risks by taking the time to evaluate situations and then anticipating what can happen when you select any of several options that may be open
- Discovering the value of homework through a simple formula for compiling facts effortlessly, learning quickly, and then applying knowledge to your advantage
- Understanding competition in such a way that it becomes a positive force in your life, not an obstacle
- Overcoming your fear of stress, which, instead of being a dangerous and disruptive force, can be controlled and made to work in your favor
- Discovering just who you are and what you are, and what your capabilities can be, in order to attain the greatest goals with the fewest restraints
- Familiarizing yourself with the "deck of cards" concept, which emphasizes that the *way* you play the cards you are dealt with in life is far more important than *what* cards you were dealt
- Understanding the nature and scope of choices, the most prevalent activity in life, and learning how to recognize them, set priorities, and bet on the right ones at the right time
- Paying true respect to history and a thorough examination of pertinent peoples and cultures faced with earth-shaking choices from earliest times to the present
- Discovering how to turn the negatives completely around and transform adversity into advantage
- Preparing yourself always to pursue the positive, at

the same time unlocking the secrets of inspiration, motivation, and productive action

The Diversity of Goals

As we have already discussed in a number of ways, Rich and Jay feel very strongly that each individual who wants to succeed in life must bring to fulfillment the best of those qualities and capabilities that already exist in their person. Comparisons can often breed discontent. So, rather than make comparisons that can place you uncomfortably in someone else's shadow, recognize from the start the fact that not everyone has—or can have—the same goals. Much unhappiness is caused by comparison. You can always find someone who is richer, better looking, more physically or mentally endowed, more well traveled, or showered with gifts that you never receive. You can make yourself miserable by comparing your lot or your achievements with those who have done better, one way or another.

Conversely, of course, people can console themselves by finding something that is worse than what they have, someone who is poorer, or people who have not been as successful. The student who gets a poor mark on an exam can always look for a classmate who has failed the exam and feel better by comparison. But this is the negative way of looking at life.

As the old adage has it, "In the world of the blind, the one-eyed man is king."

It is an exercise in frustration to start envying people who have achieved something they want that you have not attained when you know that your own goals are substantially different. It is sometimes difficult to get this message across to young people when the envy of one's classmates are too often those individuals whose families have presented them with expensive cameras, cars, or other such blunt symbols of financial success.

To develop a real faith within yourself (in addition to the more formal faith in God), you have to ask yourself, "*What is success?*" That is a short question with long answer. There is no single formula, no one little secret for achieving success, whether in business, in any other kind of endeavor, or in life itself. The results follow a pattern of activities which, if pursued and accompanied by the necessary energy, will end up as success. You also have to bring to the program a reasonable level of intelligence and knowledge to apply to your efforts.

Associating Your Work with Goals

Goals are not the end all and be all. They are basic steps to success. Furthermore, every goal that is reached has to be replaced by a new goal, otherwise your motivation ceases. If you set the goal too far out and that happens to be your only goal, then you will become discouraged before you ever reach it. The best framework for success is to set some intermediate goals that are realistic. That does not mean that you should scatter your shots in order to be sure to hit something, somewhere, somehow. The intermediate goals must line up in succession and all be aimed at the same target.

Jay Van Andel and Rich DeVos have found in their long career together that many of the goals they originally thought were unreachable were actually quite within range. The moral here is that you have to *believe* you can attain something you might not have considered earlier, if only to test and stretch your capabilities.

It is fashionable today to learn "systems" of business accomplishment, especially in the corporate world. These are expressed in books, in seminars, and other media. People rush to learn about a system and then pretty soon are dashing off in a different direction to discover a newer system that has come into vogue. Be wary about succumbing to the "systems" approach to life, realizing that "success" has many, many interpretations, depending in essence upon the individual, the location, the social structure, and dozens of other factors.

Looking at your life's goals in long range, the secret is to set and accomplish one goal at a time, then another and another. Begin right away. As many achievers have said, "Success is never achieved tomorrow. It is achieved today."

That does not mean, however, that you should confine your horizon to this present twenty-four-hour period. Ask yourself as honestly as possible, "What is my most important goal today? Tomorrow? Next week? Next month? A year from now?''

Practical goals incorporate not only a major course of action but a good many fringe activities that are necessary to the accomplishment of the whole. These are best described as ''priorities,'' since it is important to rate and rank them in terms of what has to be done, in what order, and with what degree of persistence and effort. Priorities are important in a person's life, whether in business, in family affairs, in social matters, in health programs, or in other personal activities of any real significance. Whatever you do, *stay focused.* Many people either ignore or avoid the subject of priorities because they have to make choices. They don't want to make a ''one, two, three, four. . . '' list of priorities because they are afraid they will make poor choices and put them in the wrong order of importance. Not infrequently, people put lesser options or alternatives at the head of the list—either knowingly or subconsciously—because they are afraid of overachieving or being too ambitious.

To help you effectively, priorities must be reviewed and changed periodically. Few priorities are ever constant. Young people who start a career may establish their first priority as getting hired by the right company. Once that is achieved, the top priority is no longer that one, but perhaps the chance to increase their income. And after that they may set their primary sights on promotion to a certain position, or relocation to a different city. Again, priority is a direct matter of choices—different ones for different people.

Goals have to include a ''bottom line.'' In the end, what are you going to get out of what you have set out to achieve? You certainly want to evaluate success in terms of enriching your life and finding yourself fulfilled. Too many people interpret their objectives in terms of dollars and cents.

''I want to make a million before I'm forty.''
''I want to own a big yacht and my own jet.''
''My retirement income has to be $60,000 a year.''

Despite the fluctuating trends that see young people in certain eras decrying material wealth, the desire for money is, in itself, neither a bad nor an immoral motivation. More important, of course, than what wealth can obtain is the issue of what lies beyond the acquisition of money. Money translates into a great many factors other than simply dollars and cents, or francs or pounds. It can be a house, education, food, security, status, freedom, power, or a thousand other things. Money can upgrade people, but it can also downgrade them. It can lead them into formerly unattainable fields of health, recreation, music, the arts, sports, and personal growth. It can also be the catalyst that plunges those who cannot control themselves into bouts with alcohol and drugs, the rejection of old friends, despair, and a severely distorted sense of values.

Motivation is most successful when people choose what is best for them in terms of their lives and lifestyles. We have asserted again and again to anyone who would listen that, for a great many people, it is far better for them to be the captain of a tugboat than the third mate on an ocean liner.

To carry on this simile, some people do much better in reaching their goals if they plan their lives in terms of short trips rather than long voyages. They can see more clearly where they are going and they can control their course and navigate to their destinations more accurately and reliably.

Some people also are better when they plan repetitive activities (trips) rather than a long-term project (voyage), covering the same areas again and again, instead of charting a course that leads them continually into the unknown. In this manner, they also see the same people on a regular basis and feel more comfortable and self-assured. We have discovered that, while individuals say they want to be independent, they really do not want to be alone. They are more secure, more sure of what they are doing if they have some peers and are part of a group. Few of us—even some of the most adventurous—care to set to sea as solo navigators heading for unfamiliar shores.

Someone once said that if you want to move a lot of people in a certain direction, seek out the lonely people of this world and offer them a group project that will counteract their loneliness. Relief from loneliness is a great motivator.

Put your goals on paper, along with your dreams and aspirations. Once you have expressed your aims in writing, you acknowledge the commitments and include them, both consciously and subconsciously, in your efforts. You must also, however, be honest enough to state what are you willing to sacrifice, such as hobbies and sports and recreation, in order to achieve your ends.

Failing Your Way to Success

No discussion of goals would be complete without emphasizing the fact that you have to be willing to accept failure and to understand that you are not going to achieve success overnight—not if your goals are meaningful. The paths of many notable people are paved with stepping stones that are failures before they reach their intended goals. Take a look at this miserable record of one man:

1831. He worked in a store that quickly went **out of business.**

1832. He ran for the Illinois legislature but was **defeated.**

1833. He started his own general store and **failed miserably.**

1834. He was finally elected to the Illinois legislature, but **lost bids** to become both the Speaker and the Elector.

1843. He ran for congress and **lost.**

1846. He was elected to congress but **lost his reelection bid** two years later.

1854. He campaigned for the U.S. Senate, but **was forced to withdraw.**

1858. He ran again for the Senate and **lost.**

Pretty discouraging? It might have been to most men. But the dismal record in this case was that of one of the greatest Americans of all time, Abraham Lincoln. When you think about it, almost every great or successful person's history is pockmarked with setbacks along the way. Yet it is not the failures that we remember or that are important, but the overcoming of obstacles and the ultimate success.

Rich and Jay have often said that the ability to fail is necessary to succeed. For one thing, failure is a sure sign that people have tried to surpass themselves and have dared to dream. You can actually learn valuable lessons from setbacks—lessons that you would never learn if you set your goals so low that you simply coasted smoothly along. Each disappointment teaches you something more about yourself, strengthens your resolve, and puts you closer to—not farther from—success.

Am I Making the Right Choice?

The question comes up all the time: In trying to set goals and priorities, how do I really know what is the *right* choice to make? There are so many alternatives. People are confused. We are not talking here about the lesser things in life, like trying to determine which social events to attend when there is a conflict, or which friends to send birthday cards to. Individuals are concerned—and naturally so—about choices that may make a substantial difference in the very way they are viewed by other people.

Should I quit my job and look for something better?
Should I fire a person who works for me who is not living up to expectations?
Should we stay in our present home and add some necessary improvements or should we look for a new house?

There are so many choices that affect our goals and future objectives in life that it is easy to become muddled. There is no simple rule, but what we ourselves have resolved when pushed into making choices that are really tough is to ask ourselves the leading question: Is the choice we have made one that establishes us as being responsible and realistic, or does it give the impression that we are hedging, dubious about the action we are taking?

The word *goal* is badly misunderstood by many people. It is often associated with objectives so far beyond people's realistic capabilities that they can never attain them or hope to come close. Of all the people who aspire to be president of the United States, only one will realize that goal every four years. Few will ever come close. Of those who aspire to become the head of a company or an important organization, quite a few will actually make it.

Goals for most people should be stepping stones, not some distant, hoped-for achievement. Goals should be personal and they should to some degree also be inspirational. When setting goals, ask yourself these questions:

Is the goal something I could define and describe to other people, rather than a vague kind of dream?

Is it short-range enough so I'll actually be able to chart some progress toward it in the near future?

Is it a goal I have selected because *I* want to achieve it, not because it is the "in" thing or because somebody has prodded me into it?

When I achieve that goal, what kind of satisfaction will it give me?

More importantly, how will it improve *me,* as a person?

Does the goal have enough durability so that it will retain its meaningfulness and appeal?

Many people overlook the fact that setting a goal also requires a commitment. A goal bears no resemblance to a New Year's resolution, which may or may not be kept and which, in effect, is simply a reminder that you have been failing to do something in the past but will remedy that sin of omission in the future. A goal is your commitment to *yourself.* It is a personal contract and one that may be even more important to your future than a legal contract ever could be. Goals require willpower. If you do not have the willpower to achieve the goals you want, then you have three choices:

1. Establish a different set of goals
2. Shore up your willpower
3. Abandon goal-setting completely

As a rancher friend of ours once commented, It's much easier to ride a horse in the direction the animal happens to be going.

SELF STARTER

Pause for a moment between chapters and use the time to describe on paper at least three goals you have—or should have—for the next six months.

CHAPTER
4

Choices for Body, Mind, and Soul

"I have learned from philosophers that among evils one ought not only to choose the least, but also to extract even from these any element of good that they may contain."

—Marcus Cicero

A physician who has successfully helped many people to enjoy life more fully likes to say to his patients, "Take care of your health and your health will take care of you." You don't have to be a medical expert to recognize the value of this outlook and be aware of the results. People who choose to avoid chemical dependencies of all kinds—whether alcohol, tobacco, or hard drugs—have an infinitely greater chance of living the kinds of lifestyles they want than do those who succumb habitually to the fleeting pleasures of booze, butts, and barbiturates.

Although the physician was talking specifically about physical well-being, you have to look upon health as a four-part entity that includes not only *body* but *mind, spirit,* and *emotion.* The spirit is what governs our inner selves. The mind is our talent for getting full use out of the spirit. Emotion is the energizing force that gets things done. And the body is the embodiment of mind, emotion, and spirit.

Sure, you can choose to soft-pedal your emotions. Or avoid exercising your mind too much for fear you will be classed as an intellectual. Or put a damper on exercising your muscles. Or repress your spirit so that you will be more of a low-key character. But the individuals who choose to give equal billing to all four parts of their personalities are the ones who are likely to live richer, more balanced lives.

Young people did not worry much about health twenty-five or thirty years ago, certainly not the way they do today. Health has become a youth-oriented factor in life and has affected not only the lifestyles of younger people but also the outlooks of older people who can see the beneficial results. This trend has substantially influenced young people in their choice of careers. They see certain industries or companies as being health-oriented or environmentally aware and they favor that direction. Going back many years, we have always been convinced that the person who observes the basic rules of good nutrition and exercise and other activities necessary to optimize health is likely, under normal conditions, to go farther than the person who does not recognize these factors. You are only as good as the health of your body and mind.

The tragedy of today's society is that too many people, the young particularly, destroy the greatest tool they have—their brains—with drugs. They literally soak their brain cells with chemicals and make it impossible for them to function effectively. Making the unfortunate choice to go the drug route quickly results in a situation where there no longer is any choice. By the time the users of drugs decide they want to quit, the damage has been done. They may become deeply involved in a spiritual program and even help others to avoid the same deadly route, but they will never achieve what they had chosen to accomplish originally.

Focusing your energy is an important adjunct to success. You cannot effectively bring all of your energy, physiological and psychological alike, to bear on an endeavor without making serious choices. Why? Because you have to make choices about the steps you will take and the order in which they will be outlined. Rich and Jay learned this lesson years ago when they were trying to establish their careers and create the businesses that would achieve their objectives. "We could select the things we wanted to do," explains Jay, "but it was much more difficult to choose the order in which we wanted to undertake them. One method we used was that of jotting down individual essentials in our overall plans on file cards and then putting the cards in sequence. Thus, we prioritized our objectives and, if we found that priorities changed, we could always change the positions of the cards."

Prioritize your choices in everything you do that is important. But, equally important, do not hesitate to change the sequence periodically.

SELF STARTER

Make a list of what you consider to be your top priorities as far as your health is concerned. How have these changed in the past five years, if at all?

Be Healthy—Physically, Mentally, Emotionally

Your body is special. The greatest asset you have is your own body, including your mind and your spirit. Retaining good health is a very important factor in determining how far you will progress and how much you will achieve in life. You do not have to be a rugged specimen or capable of all kinds of athletic feats, but simply be as trim and fit as possible, and able to maintain a positive outlook and carry enthusiasm into everything you do. The most important thing is that, in the course of evaluating yourself and your potential, you must make an honest appraisal of the state of your health—physical, mental, and emotional—and what you can do to improve it and maintain it. In the end, it is a great deal better to choose to live a healthy and productive life than to talk about it.

People are more and more concerned about old age, too, because there is no doubt that Americans are getting older and senior citizens have every right to want to choose what they can do when they are in their seventies and eighties rather than being relegated to some kind of institution. They are typified by the older citizen who made an appointment with his doctor for a checkup because he wasn't feeling up to par.

"You realize," said the doctor after he had made the usual tests and found nothing seriously wrong, "that there is nothing I can do to make you feel younger."

"It isn't that I want to be younger," replied the patient, "I just want to make sure I keep getting older."

When you are young, you have the choice of what you will do to assure that you get older gracefully and comfortably. But by the time you are older, there may not be too much choice left. "We owe much of our own success to the fact that we have lived our lives in moderation physically, are not at all self-conscious about revealing ourselves emotionally, and have always felt that our spiritual selves need just as much regular nourishment as do our bodies," says Rich. "Tied in with the balance of health is an outlook which recognizes that nothing can ever be perfect and people should learn to live with problems as well as with satisfactions. There is no need to react adversely to a reversal by becoming undone. People like that are usually failures, in business or anything else."

The healthiest reaction is to take a positive stand, adds Jay, no matter how distressing things may look at the moment. "How do we fix this? Where do we go from here?" If a wheel falls off, put it back on and keep going.

Resilience is one of the most enviable qualities in people who are healthy in mind, body, and spirit and is a vital factor in achieving goals. People who observe the rules of good nutrition and exercise and take steps to optimize their health are likely to have this quality of resilience, be more successful, and enjoy life more fully than those who do not. The process includes exercise of the brain as well, and encouraging attitudes that help to preserve your mental health. One of the great tragedies of today's society is the ready access to drugs of all kinds, legal and illegal alike.

Why do people get hooked on drugs? There are no pat answers for such a complex problem. But one common reason is certainly fear—the fear of failure, or not being accepted, or facing real and imagined threats. Dr. Norman Vincent Peale told us that the two most powerful words in any language were *faith* and *fear*. Faith can move mountains and fear can shatter you. As he explained, there are five ways to combat fear: Believe in yourself; associate with confident people; tune up your confidence machine; be master of your ship; and keep busy.

It is a surprising truth that all of these actions are also steps to good health and success.

To these actions, you should add one more: **Exercise enthusiasm because enthusiasm is good exercise.**

The fact of the matter is that what people possess in the way of money and power and material goods may provide little comfort in the face of personal problems and aspirations. Nothing can convince a person of the inadequacy of money so fast as having a lot of it! Those who acquire fortunes soon discover how limited money can be. It cannot buy peace of mind. Or heal ruptured relationships. Or impart meaning to a life that has none. Or relieve guilt or a broken heart.

That is not to say that material things should all be regarded as anti-spiritual. Everything on earth is material, including the clothing worn by a minister of the church and the Bible itself. Although we should not worship money, we can enjoy the fruits of our labors, the material things, without being evil. You can be successful without compromising your faith and your belief in God.

In addition to faith, energy is a key because without it nothing happens, no matter how auspicious the other ingredients may be. Success is made possible by a kind of multicolored rope, whose threads are all woven together to provide the necessary strength to pull you ahead of the crowd.

The Three A's: Attitude, Action, Atmosphere

In line with the positive attitude that this book is espousing, Rich DeVos asserts that these are great days in which we live—the best of times, even though some people groan that it is the worst of times.

> Despite the fears of the naysayers, the country in general and most communities as a part of the whole are in fine shape. Most people enjoy decent jobs; spendable income is up; inflation has been held in check; and there are more opportunities—economically, socially, recreationally, culturally, and spiritually than in any other nation in the world.
>
> As we like to say in our own business, "Let us run while others walk."
>
> In every major venture there is a tripartite pattern that we refer to as "The Three A's," which influences the turn of events and the people who participate in those events:
>
> *Action* is the goal on which we set our sights, whether we are selling products, trying to influence people to reach certain decisions, planning the construction of a large building, supporting the arts, running for public office, or becoming involved in almost any other field of human endeavor.

Attitude fits quickly into place because much of the success of achieving action depends upon our attitudes. Even when raising young children, you can demand an action, but the demand grows weaker and weaker as they grow older unless positive attitudes have been molded. What we do in effect is to try to reinforce an attitude that achieves the ends we cannot force by taking action.

We may not be able to force action, so we turn to attitude. We have a little better chance of motivating someone to do something if we can mold an attitude or attitudes. No matter how constructive or great we think our attitudes are, we can hope for no more than to convince other people that we are right. But we cannot force them to think that way. Giving a sense of confidence is one means of helping to shape attitudes. But one person cannot tell other persons that their attitudes *must* be such and such.

Atmosphere is the third leg of the triangle and the only one of the three that we can control. Once you understand this, you will stop trying to force action or change attitudes. Atmosphere is what provides the motivation for attitudes and actions. When we are fully aware of the power of atmosphere, then we can use it to influence the first two elements, Action and Attitude.

We grow up in different communities—"atmospheres" if you will—some of us in favorable ones, which were basically beneficial, others in unpleasant atmospheres, which tended to foster disharmonies and regrets.

As DeVos points out, you can come from a poor family and live in a modest house with few amenities. Yet the atmosphere can be positive and uplifting—what some refer to as "good air." No matter what endeavor you undertake, if you get people to breathe the right air, then that atmosphere becomes a strong, positive force in moving people and motivating them. This quality is particularly valuable in community work and in helping participants to associate more strongly and productively with their communities.

Mission, Message, and Method

"We don't necessarily try to insist that all good and beneficial
forces are triple functions," says Jay,

> but the "Three M's" are very meaningful to us—as
> much as the "Three A's" when we try to describe how
> a successful, well managed company can best serve its
> employees and the public. In our case, we think of our-
> selves and our associates not just as people helping peo-
> ple but as people helping people to help themselves. That
> is the mission. The message is that we can show you how
> to help yourself. And the method is very simple: com-
> munication by demonstration. It does no one much good
> to be told something if that something cannot also be
> demonstrated.
>
> In the world today, we see too many governments at
> all levels which function on the premise that people are
> incapable of helping themselves and therefore have to be
> helped. No one has any choice in the matter. As a result,
> the huge financial burden of establishing and maintaining
> social agencies becomes so top-heavy that chaos results.

Several years ago an advertisement for a hospital dramati-
cally and graphically reflected this outlook and perhaps could
even echo a cry of hope around the world. The ad told the
story of an obese man named David who fell against a plate
glass window when the stepladder on which he was working
broke under his great weight. When the window shattered, the
glass severed the tendons in his wrists so that he could not
use his hands. After a long and very complicated operation,
when it seemed that he might never regain any muscle control,
a nurse told him that the surgeons and the hospital had done

all they could physically but now they would help him to help himself.

David ultimately discovered that he could not only regain the use of his hands but that he could start taking control of himself. He managed to trim his weight from about 300 pounds to 165 and, as a result of his new attitude and understanding, started a business and changed his whole life.

This is one of the finest examples we know of people helping people to help themselves.

Action and Reaction

We do not have to look very far to find success stories, whether of the heartwarming variety like David's or examples of people who had unusual goals and pursued them to fruition. Our newspapers and magazines and television screens are filled with such stories. Many provide inspiration for other people who would like to emulate them. The recognition of success, however, is just the first step on the road to achievement. Many people spend most of their lifetime reading about the accomplishments of men and women in a wide variety of fields until they practically become experts on success formulas. Yet they never achieve success themselves because they simply do not make the effort. It is futile to complain about your lot in life if the only action you have taken is with your mouth. Many people never find out how well they could do in a venture because all they do is talk about what might have been.

These people are the "If Onlys." If only I had done this, or that, or something else, just look where I'd be! They are the types whose comments about life start out with the words, "One of these days. . . "

Well, "one of these days" is *gone* and you had better get on with some kind of action or else shut up! It is not only frustrating but often pathetic to see how many people dream about what might happen but then never discipline themselves to try to do something. There is always a reason why it's not going to happen this week, but some time in the future, "As soon as. . . "

What these people badly need is not aspiration or inspiration, but an old-fashioned kick in the pants!

We also need to respect the value of human energy in the equation of success. Thomas A. Edison once remarked, "Genius is one percent inspiration and ninety-nine percent perspiration." Unfortunately, too many people have heard this so often in school that they hardly deign to consider it today.

Always bear in mind that, in the entire world, there is no one else exactly like you. Accept the person you are, not in a sedentary fashion but with a resolve to improve the image. Nothing happens until you yourself do something. Success is always out there waiting for you. But it is you who have to go and claim it.

Too many people live their lives as if to protect the past. They live in a self-created forest where all they can see are the trees.

What they need most of all in order to escape from their confined environment and see what life can really offer is to develop the kinds of choices we have been talking about, to establish strong, positive links to themselves, their families, their friends and associates, an established faith, the community, the nation, their work, and to those forces of inspiration that will convert plans into actions.

Beware the Comfort Zone

Quite a few of us who have served in the military can sympathize with the account of a young man who had recently become a second lieutenant in the army. When he asked how and why he had made the long jump from private to officer, he replied,

> Well, it all started one day when I was a bare-faced recruit. I was out on a hot, dusty field in the middle of summer marching back and forth until we had no more sweat left in our bodies. And as we staggered along the edge of the parched training field, we passed the officer's quarters where a couple of lieutenants were sitting in the shade imbibing cool drinks.
>
> That was where I wanted to be, not down on the sun-baked earth working my butt off. I knew there was a long

period of hard labor and education ahead of me, but I was willing to undergo the rigors in order to reach that goal.

The arrival is fun, but many parts of the trip are not. In selling, for example, forcing yourself to get out of the office or your home to get moving and look for prospective customers is not easy. Even the best salespeople admit to letting themselves get bogged down in "the comfort zone" sometimes, rather than stirring themselves into action. No matter what career you may be pursuing, the routines in life tend to be the comfort zones that run counter to your goals.

Those who succeed find that they have to resort to a number of little tricks to keep themselves motivated because once they get going and overcome the inertia, they are more readily able to keep up the momentum. It is always so easy to tell yourself that this is not really the right time for action. It's too hot. Or too cold. Or your horoscope is not quite right.

The popularity of an activity can be one method—a "trick" if you will—of avoiding the comfort zone. The mind-set of a community can influence people. Take jogging, for example, or vigorous daily walks. It was easy to avoid such forms of exertion during an era in which people tended to laugh at those who were jogging buffs or health nuts. But once this form of exercise became acceptable and then popular, it in itself became a kind of comfort zone in which many people felt right at home.

SELF STARTER

List three tricks or devices you use to keep yourself motivated or to start on a project you have been putting off for too long a time.

Personal Discipline

An important choice you have to make regards discipline. You can be easy on yourself or you can be tough on yourself. If you choose to be lax, everything you do is likely to fit that same pattern. If you exert proper discipline, your body and mental attitudes will reflect that and you are much more likely to get jobs done, avoid procrastination, and really get to enjoy what you are doing.

It is much like going out for a sport. You end up getting out of it exactly what you put into it. If you will condition your body to the requirements of the sport (or job), you will be rewarded with many more satisfactions than if you elect to follow the lazy route, sit back, and let others take over.

Evaluate your time and analyze how much you devote to "accentuating the positive." Discipline becomes very important as you mature because it develops good habits and contributes to your ability to learn. Your appearance is important, too, and discipline can help to keep you slim, in good health, and vigorous. If you forfeit discipline, you are more than likely to slip into sloppy ways—in all departments.

One problem that we all face regularly is to get down to the things we have to do. The first step in overcoming this very human weakness is to recognize the fact that discipline is not easy. No matter who you are or where you are or how smart you are, discipline is against human nature. So you are already fighting the system, as it were.

The second step is to understand that a good many disciplines are established early in life. Going to church, for example, is a discipline that some people have and others do not. Changes in discipline are likely to occur when there are crises—a panic, an epidemic, a scare—brought on by a serious threat to your health, or perhaps poverty or hunger or family emotional upheavals.

What are some of the events that cause people to sit back and reconsider their lives and their activities? They might include a death in the family, the case of a son or daughter who leaves home abruptly under bitter circumstances, or a health episode that makes one think more seriously about weight, diet, and lifestyle.

Some psychologists call these *trigger points.*

They are the events or circumstances that make people change their viewpoints and habits, that make them finally come round to disciplining themselves in order to counteract the problems or threats.

If you have trouble with discipline, there are certain tricks you can use to fool yourself into taking proper action. Among these are:

- Blocking out a period of time each day in which to complete a set chore
- Working with other people so that all of you are involved in something that has to be done, or should be done, regularly
- Keeping a score card on activities like exercise or diet or task performance
- Giving yourself some kind of reward each time you complete a certain routine
- Taping a picture in a prominent place (such as the refrigerator) to depict something that you will be rewarded with if you discipline yourself properly
- Making a boring routine more exciting through the use of some kind of gimmick

People are often too impatient to impose proper discipline on themselves. They ignore the fact that it often takes a long time to establish a solid pattern, sometimes years, whereas a lot of people think they are going to do that in a week or a month. You see this all the time with people who go on diets. They diet for sixty days and lose weight and then within thirty more days they have put it all back on. Why? Because they never really did establish the pattern so that it would work.

Jay Van Andel and Rich DeVos have found that one of the most effective forms of self-discipline is working with other people. When working in a group, you can accomplish some things more easily and continually than when trying to do it by yourself. Doing things with other people is one definite form of motivation. You don't have to go to college at all, for example, to acquire knowledge that can be learned through printed books and videotapes and audiotapes. But when you go to college you become part of a group and the studying becomes more palatable than doing it all by yourself, as a loner. With the kinds of visual aids we have today for home study, there is no reason why an entire education cannot be acquired at home. But few people have the discipline to do this effectively.

We mentioned reducing boredom as an antidote to some chore that was necessary but boring. A good example is the stationary bicycle that was invented as a handy way of getting exercise similar to bicycling down the street, but without having to leave the house, dress properly, or face inclement weather. The problem was that this kind of pedaling was nowhere near as interesting as riding along a highway or path where there was something to see. So people used the device of watching television, reading books, or listening to music and audio programs on tape as they worked off the calories in the privacy of their homes.

When you are in business for yourself, as an entrepreneur, you need different disciplines to keep motivated. It becomes very important to become disciplined because you don't have people telling you when to do things or setting deadlines. You are your own taskmaster. When you are working in a structured business, you just have to do what you are supposed to do or eventually you will be fired. Also, you have to go to a certain place regularly and follow certain patterns of work and responsibility. The discipline is set for you. Without having developed the pattern of doing things when you have your own business, you will fail. You have to evolve a routine. It always helps to have two or more people working together because teamwork is an effective form of discipline.

If you can provide reinforcement for your goals and get family members involved, you may proceed faster. You should also have a way of rewarding yourself when you do attain a goal, or step toward a goal. If you lose a certain number of pounds, say, or reach a stage in some other form of self-improvement, acknowledge it. It helps here, of course, to have children or other family members who share in the rewards or at least can cheer you on.

Beauty Is as Beauty Does

A lot of people—too many in fact—lose all sense of discipline and motivation because they say that they are not as attractive as other people.

"No wonder Joe gets all the breaks," they say. "He's handsome and personable."

Or, "I can see why Sally gets chosen for the best assignments. She's pretty and knows how to turn on the charm."

Beauty gets cited erroneously for worlds of a things it does not deserve. "Beauty" is another one of those popular words that is both overvalued and misunderstood. People tend to become almost neurotic about the matter of being beautiful. Some of the world's most enormous businesses are based on catering to the millions upon millions of people who want to achieve good looks. That is all well and good. There is nothing wrong with trying to look your best, an exemplary action when not carried to extremes.

The problem here lies in the fact that people often do not appreciate inner beauty in others or try to develop it in themselves. Reflect on those qualities within you that you can most easily perfect by asking yourself a few direct questions:

What are some of my best qualities and traits as a person?
Which of these qualities can I improve most easily?
What are some of the traits I should be wary about and get rid of as best I can?
Who are some of the people I know who have inner beauties I would like to emulate?

One interpretation of inner beauty is *spirituality,* defined as relating to the spirit or soul rather than one's physiological or physical nature. Yet some people fear this elusive quality, connecting it erroneously with matters like spiritualism and superstition. You do not have to be religious to possess a positive kind of spirituality, although it is evident that many people who adhere strongly to a religious faith also possess an inner spiritual beauty. In choosing a faith to help guide themselves, they also make it easier to understand and develop this kind of spirituality.

Harmony of body, mind, and soul can work wonders for a person's growth and enrichment of life. Again, though, it is a matter of choices. You have all seen athletes who have spent so much time perfecting their physical entities that their brains have atrophied and their souls were left far behind during the race for physical supremacy. At the other end of the pole, you are certainly familiar with so-called intellectuals who are all brains and whose bodies are puny and in the eyes of some people almost repugnant.

If you cannot change your face, at least you can change your mind and your relationships with people. When you get right down to it, some relationships are really beautiful and transcend physical elements, while others can be brutal, even if the people involved are good looking and perhaps personable as well.

SELF STARTER

Picture in your mind two people you know who are physically beautiful, but are unattractive from a personality standpoint. How about two others who are just the reverse?

Very few people are really ugly. The problem with most people who think they are not beautiful is that they have done nothing to highlight or emphasize their strong points. You can improve yourself 100 percent just by taking steps to be cleaner, to dress better, or to use makeup properly. Most people who are called ugly or homely are not really that way at all—they just haven't learned how to take care of themselves physically or how to react mentally and emotionally. A smile can be better than the finest makeup in improving someone's personality and looks.

Don't forget that your self-esteem is important, too. If you comport yourself and carry yourself with assurance and dignity, you will impress people as being physically attractive as well.

We can apply the beauty incentive to some of the concepts of discipline that we have been talking about. Weight, for instance, is certainly an element of beauty. You can choose any of a number of ways to enhance your personal image, your looks, how you take care of personal cleanliness, do your hair, and in other ways make yourself more attractive. So many people fall into the habit of being just plain sloppy and lazy. They stay up late watching television or having a few drinks at a bar and in the morning are just plain too tired to take care of what should be done. Time is very important in any form of discipline and the enhancement of the self—what you do and when you do it.

We have discovered that personal perception prevents a lot of people from improving their looks. The images they have of themselves, that "I don't look good," or "I can't ever do anything with my hair or my big nose," even though often voiced humorously, prevent people from doing anything constructive to improve themselves. So you have to change that perception and say to yourself, "Boy, I really *do* look good, if I'll take care of myself and follow a daily routine of constant self-improvement."

Money serves as a perpetual excuse for many people. They claim that they are too poor and have no budget for proper clothes. Yet there are plenty of examples of people who have acquired a knack for finding appropriate clothing at bargain prices or who know what to do with hand-me-downs to improve their appearance. Economics, unfortunately, serves as a widespread excuse for not doing a lot of things.

Physical beauty alone is not always an asset. It may be an advantage at first, as in the case of a lovely young lady who is trying to land a good job and make an impression in some kind of career. Yet not a few women who are physically well endowed start relying on beauty as a means of getting what they want out of life and when the physical beauty fades they are left with nothing to fall back on as a driving force. They fail to exercise their brains and develop their talents.

What you choose to look like can, in the long run, decisively affect your personality and your ability to achieve, but above all, you must have faith in yourself and a vision of what you want to be. "Getting a new vision is something all of us need from time to time," writes Jim Counihan in his daily guide to successful living, *Another Step.*

When B. P. Burkland was born he had polio and couldn't walk or crawl as a baby. His parents carried him around in a little wooden box. Then one day, when he was a little boy, they stood him up before a mirror. When he saw himself standing up, looking like other boys, he began to move his arms and legs. He got a new vision of himself and never went into the box again. Eventually, it changed his life and he became one of the wealthiest men in America. He says, "My mission is to tell people, you don't have to live in a box." You don't have to, either. Get a new vision!

CHAPTER
5

Options Governing the Business of Living

"The measure of choosing well is whether a man
likes and finds good in what he has chosen."

—Charles Lamb

Once you learn how to choose your goals so that you can associate your aspirations with yourself, you will be far more likely to understand other people. You will learn, for example, how to communicate with others, not only by your personal expression but by cultivating the power to listen. Because you have already focused time and attention on the objective of finding out who you are and what you hope to do, you will find it easier to discover exactly who other people are and accept them for what they are, and then communicate. Knowing your audience gives you an edge when you are trying to communicate. When you show interest and honest understanding, you then earn the right to be heard. But remember that knowing how to say something is one thing—having something to say is quite another.

Never be afraid to speak up. Communication is a critical element in maintaining strong associations, with your inner self to begin with and with other people, whether they are close to you or are strangers.

It is a strange truth, but you can voice almost any opinion, no matter how controversial, as long as you do so with respect.

Rich DeVos says,

We like young people who have high levels of aspiration; who are communicators; who have a solid religious foundation; who know who they are and what their lives are based on; who are encouragers and who talk positively and avoid the endless—and mindless—moaning and groaning about what's wrong with society and the whole world. We like young people who are able to look more at what's right and what can be accomplished than at the things that are wrong and are sure to tear us all down.

We know only too well the youths who make nasty remarks at people who have certain possessions they wished they had. "Why don't you give your money to the poor?" they taunt, making snide comments about your car or house or other material evidence of success. Most likely, they pick this up from their own parents, who were the original naysayers and critics of those who possessed more than they did. They try to inflate their own lives and egos by tearing other people down.

They can never be in a position of leadership because they are too filled with the negatives—envy, jealousy, hatred—to aim at goals that are positive and constructive.

People need a feeling of involvement in order to reach goals and be achievers, along with a sense of self-importance (in the positive meaning of the word). Oftentimes this can be accomplished through very simple acts of sympathy for others, kindness, and understanding. We talk about people who are successful because they have a certain charisma. Most often that characteristic is little more than paying attention to the needs and problems of others and being supportive—sometimes verbally, sometimes through small acts.

People say they like small towns because they experience this feeling of involvement more easily than they do in cities. But remember that a city is not a *thing*—it's hundreds of thousands, perhaps millions, of people who are living and functioning just as individually as the citizens of small towns. Number yourself among those who are constructive by contributing to charities and cultural groups, by cleaning up litter, speaking well of your neighborhood, talking about it—and your job—with pride, telling everyone that this is a great place to live and you are going to help keep it that way.

SELF STARTER

List three things you have done to help your neighbors and neighborhood in the past year. Then list three other things you might do to help build a sense of pride.

John W. Galbreath, one of the most successful men in America, once remarked, "If you don't love people, you can have all the college degrees in the world and you'll never be a success."

Human Dignity

Some time ago, the Dutch government set up a program for artists whereby they were put on the government payroll and asked to produce art in exchange for salaries. But the government then put all of the art in warehouses and very little of it was ever seen by the public. The artists, despite the fact that they were getting paid, were displeased with the program. Money might have been necessary to them, but it was not as important as their creative production of something of value and, as far as they could see, the works were not judged to be valuable enough to be recognized and publicly displayed.

This unfortunate case is a good example of one of the basic needs of human dignity and the realization of the value of mutual self-respect. The most important commodity in the world is respect for the individual—not an abstract, purely intellectual kind of respect for mankind, but an active, daily awareness of the worth of every person, regardless of color, creed, station in life, or other conditions.

Today, we use too many false judgments, based on job status, education achieved, social standing, physical virility, and wealth.

"He's *just* a mechanic."
"She's *just* a housewife."
"They are *just* farmers."

If you take this attitude, you are denying the human dignity of millions of people who form the backbone of the nation.

We could carry this attitude to outlandish extremes. "He's just a Ph.D.," implying that he's a nerd for spending all that time studying when he could have done something practical. "He's just a senator," implying that he and his ilk are bags of hot air. "He's just a multimillionaire," basking in bundles of money instead of being a minister or doing something useful for society.

Today, salesmanship is often panned, especially by people who forget that America has become great because of the people who worked hard to sell the products and services that have made the country what it is.

It's time to get off each other's backs, to get out of everyone's hair, to quit the petty sniping and bickering about this group and that group. To stop playing one-upmanship. Let us now give each other respect.

When was the last time you thanked the teacher for putting up with your kids' faults? Or the community volunteer who has worked tirelessly at the hospital? Or the political candidates who ran and lost, after committing long hours and money to causes in which they believed?

Do the people you associate with daily really know that you respect them? And do they, in return, express their honest respect for *you?*

Timeliness is also an important element in the manner in which you are viewed by other people. The image of almost any type of career you can mention rises and falls in the public eye, depending to a large degree on what has been accomplished recently by people in that field—or, conversely, what has been done to demean a profession. If you are trying to zero in on a choice of career, for example, you will find that there are various stages that are important in the progression. The timing may not always be within your control. Sometimes things just happen. Sometimes people launch themselves at fortuitous moments while others are not so fortunate. So you have to recognize what is, or is not, within your direct control.

It is, unfortunately, often easier just to put off any decision for the moment. "I'd better get around to that later," young people frequently say, "after I see what happens. When I find myself."

Faith makes it easier for you to do what you have to do today instead of procrastinating. There is an old Spanish adage about the common practice of putting things off: "Tomorrow is the busiest day of the week." Do what you intend to do now because if you don't do it, then you've lost this day forever.

Procrastination is often utilized as the solution for people who have some unpleasant task to perform, which of course they have placed at the end of their list of things to do. Have enough faith in yourself to try this formula: The first person to call or write or see is the one you are most afraid of or skeptical about. Once you have hurdled that obstacle, all the rest of the things on your list will be easier than you could have imagined.

> **SELF STARTER**
> Ask yourself what, of all the things you have put off this month, is the most threatening or distasteful. Then take care of it—now.

The Secret of Dialogue

A great many people are known as talkers. You hear them all the time, ranging from the constant chatterers to those who sound like experts on a wide variety of current topics. Yet very few of these people really know how to carry on a *dialogue*. They are talkers, but not communicators.

Dialogue is all-important in your association with your family, your friends, and your community. Listening to what others have to say, as well as getting your own message across, can often make the difference between the success or failure of a proposed program or plan of action. Communication is a proclamation of connectedness among all humans. No matter how worthy your intentions or wonderful your message, the value of your communication—the degree to which you show that you care—depends upon the impact with which it is received at the other end.

Billy Graham has said, "The greatest public enemy is not the Mafia or Communism, but indifference." To illustrate how critically young people in particular need to be included in regular family dialogue, he told a story about World War II. During the period when England was being heavily bombed by German aircraft, many parents in London sent their children to safer locations in the distant countryside. But social studies made after the war showed that the children who remained in London with their parents, where they had the emotional security of regular communication and understanding, were less disturbed—despite the bombings—than those for whom the choice was made to send them to safety.

We can all use better communication in peacetime as well as wartime. In America, we need a continuing dialogue with our country as well as with each other. One of the most rewarding and significant choices all Americans can have is to associate their philosophies of life with their nation. As the old adage has it, "If you want to be a winner, stick with the winners." America is the greatest winner in the history of mankind and the people who link themselves closely and firmly to what America has to offer are the ones who will come out ahead in the long run.

Unfortunately, too few people understand this dynamic relationship. At worst, they negate it; at best, they simply overlook the opportunities.

The situation is comparable to that of the man who decided that he would sell his home. The realtor he selected prepared an advertisement and ran it in the local newspaper. The next day, the home owner rushed into the real estate office, holding a clipping from the paper in hand.

"Please take my house off the market," he fairly shouted. "Right away!"

"But why?" asked the perplexed realtor.

"Because," came the reply, "After I read your ad, I realized I already own the kind of house I really want to live in!"

In a nutshell, that is the story of America. People live and work in its cities and towns from coast to coast without ever realizing that they are citizens of the greatest country in the world. Don't sell America short! To the contrary, tap the very richness of its roots and you'll learn how to find great nourishment and strength by associating yourself with your own country. That is one of your inalienable rights and a force that can be very powerful in helping you shape a better lifestyle and assure yourself of a more meaningful future.

If you want to choose those values that are positive, productive, and enduring, you can do no better than to proclaim your sense of loyalty to America. That does not mean that you have to take a Pollyannaish stand and accept everything American as being perfect and beyond reproach. There are plenty of valid things to criticize about the country from almost any viewpoint one wants to select—governmental, financial, social, ethical, cultural—you name it. But many critics—too often in high places—zero in on minor flaws and present major denouncements that are totally out of context.

Influential voices even went so far at one time as to downgrade the country by comparing its works with some of the so-called breakthroughs achieved by the Russians. One answer to that argument was very simple: If we in America wanted to enjoy the glories of the Soviet system, as some had suggested, we could have done so by getting along on one-third of our natural gas, ripping up more than 90 percent of our paved highways and two-thirds of our railroad tracks, scrapping nineteen out of every twenty of our cars and trucks, and closing about 85 percent of our museums. In effect, we could have simulated the Russians quite easily by cutting our living standards by two-thirds.

The Spirit of America

As Rich and Jay point out again and again to the public in their speeches and articles, what really makes the nation strong is not a bundle of statistics, but the spirit of America, an essence that in itself is often a derisive target of those who are adept at putting down people and goals.

What is this spirit?

It is many elements and ideas molded into one concept that establishes the tone and sets the country apart from all other peoples. It is expressed in the message on the Statue of Liberty itself, which addresses itself to all those "yearning to breathe free," to taste the fullness of life, to plot an independent course.

We can thank America's forefathers for pioneering when they tore the concept of inferiority to shreds and made a shambles of the negative approach to life and freedom. We can thank them, too, for having the foresight to realize that the real strength of the nation lay in the faith of its citizens and in its rich religious tradition. Too many people lose sight of the fact that America is what it is today because God has blessed this land. Faith in God is the real secret of the American dream and one that every individual can tap in order to gain personal strength and vigor.

As every dollar bill proclaims, "In God we trust."

When the noted Philippine patriot, Carlos P. Romulo, returned home after seventeen years in the United States as an ambassador and one of the founders of the United Nations, he said as he departed, "It is this respect for the dignity of the human spirit which makes America invincible....May God keep you always—and may you always keep God."

The Richness of Expanded Viewpoints

Open your mind to the unbelievable resources that are part of the American heritage and you open the door to inner powers of your own that you did not even know existed. Too many of us live in watertight compartments; we live parcels of life, rather than the whole.

Our sense of time and timing is a good example. We proclaim that we are going to accomplish this or that in thirty days or sixty days or a year. But often our long-term goals are overshadowed by our short-term commitments, those day-to-day activities that seem so important. Similarly, we can lose sight of the positive aspects of our nation if we spend most of our time complaining about those specific problems that plague us for the moment.

We live today in a world in which people have come to expect everything instantly. The fast-food business is so ingrained that we become impatient, even nervous, if we do not get served right away. Many new businesses are focused on instant expectations. Success is expected to come quickly and not a few businesses fail because their founders do not give them a long enough chance to mature.

Nevertheless, when you get right down to it, at every level, American commerce is truly remarkable. Unlike many conditions abroad, our telephone network is dependable; banks or automatic banking systems are open seven days a week around the clock; factories produce on orderly schedules; the buses roll; medicine continues to achieve wondrous breakthroughs; we enjoy a constant and seldom interrupted flow of energy; and science devises great works that were unheard of a few years ago. Even the postal system, described as ponderous and in some instances unreliable, achieves records of delivery on the poorest of its days that are unrivaled abroad under the most fortunate circumstances.

Our greatest asset in America is *people*. They are not perfect, but for all our faults, America has become the most people-oriented nation on earth and we should thank the multitudes of citizens who make it possible and recognize its wonders. Be proud to link yourself with and be part of this system which, after all, is less than 400 years old.

SELF STARTER

List three advantages Americans have over people living in other countries. Can you list any disadvantages?

What does the future hold? As Americans, we live in a free society where we have the option to try, continually, new ways and means. You don't need all the answers to get in the swim—just the gumption to start paddling when you hit the water!

Free men keep producing. That's why the American farmer puts lights on his machines and works into the night, while the Communist farmer calls it a day before sundown and could not care less about personal productivity. Despite occasional, and sometimes deserved, outcries of government intervention, agriculture has played a steady and reliable part in America's role of leadership through many generations. If you want to know what really happens when government gets out of control, think of the sad plight of Argentina. Once among the greatest food-producing nations in the world, it slipped to the point of beggarly dependency on food from outside its borders after the government slapped on price controls and tried to dictate how farmers should function.

If you choose to involve yourself in activities related to the remarkable resources that make up America and the spirit of America, you will have strong creative and productive forces working constantly to your advantage.

Whether you are involved with a full-time job to which you

commute, work at home in a casual style, hold a number of volunteer jobs, are retired, or are still young enough to be trying to plan a meaningful career, there is one aspect of your life that is as essential as the air you breathe and the water you drink: *work.* "To have nothing to do," said a noted philosopher, "is to be nothing."

We cannot address ourselves to all of the categories of work that exist in the nation, but we can use one of the most powerful examples of all time to demonstrate how people can associate themselves with the right concept of rewarding labor to their great and enduring advantage: free enterprise.

The Miracle of Free Enterprise

Few of the nation's leaders are more vociferous than the DeVos/Van Andel team in asserting that "the most-ignored blessing and advantage of the American way of life is free enterprise. We take it for granted. Some critics even go so far as to denigrate it as a 'capitalistic' social flaw. Yet the free enterprise system is the greatest single source of the economic success of America, or any society or nation that lets it function unshackled."

Too many people look upon free enterprise as an issue that is unimportant in their lives, something best left to the economists and political scientists to quibble over. To the contrary, however, it is a concept that occurs when the freedom of people is recognized as an inherent right, to be safeguarded in the structure of the nation's government. It is a system that lets us be free to own our tools and equipment, risk our money and time, make our own business decisions, and experience profits or losses in accordance with our abilities and endeavors.

Critics of the system claim that it is a lopsided and biased scheme whereby the rich grow richer and the poor get poorer. What they don't realize is that the poor are not going to get any richer if the rich get poorer. In fact, they will end up having even less.

Incentive and leadership are two of the fundamental keys to free enterprise. The incentive lies not only in material rewards for the work we have done, but in a number of intangibles, not the least of which is the satisfaction for having achieved certain goals and often the recognition of others for what we have accomplished.

Leadership is not always easy to define. What are the qualities of a *leader?* They are many, including talent, intelligence, and hard work. But first and foremost, the most important quality of leaders is that they have respect for other people.

Leadership is more than authority over people or the professional abilities and skills to achieve technical goals. Being a leader is being the kind of person that others want to follow or emulate—getting the job done through people.

Leadership also implies the capacity and desire to work hard to achieve objectives. As poet and dramatist Ben Jonson said back in the seventeenth century, ''What is written without effort is generally read without pleasure.'' If you are afraid to work more than eight hours a day, don't even start out to try to improve your situation. Do all the things that you like to do that while away the time and give you pleasure, but then don't cry because other people get the promotions, make higher incomes, and have more than you do.

Personal Rewards

One of the advantages enjoyed by people who choose to live in a free-enterprise kind of environment is that their benefits and rewards are greater and more meaningful. Material rewards are incentives that fuel the free-enterprise society. People are effectively motivated, not by force, but by solid compensation for achievement, which may be in the form of money, status, recognition, or simply the realization of goals.

How many of these priorities could be delegated to others? Learning how to delegate is one important formula for success and is one that, again, depends directly on the matter of choice. Without selecting qualified, efficient, and well oriented associates, you simply cannot delegate anything. If you are selling products or services, for example, and it is more important for you to spend time actually making contacts and generating sales, then you should delegate less important, but time-consuming, functions to others—bookkeeping, for instance.

''If you are running an inn,'' says DeVos,

you had better spend most of your time out front with
your paying guests and delegate the housekeeping, cook-
ing, and services to your staff. As we mentioned earlier,
when we were first starting in business together, we op-
erated a flying school. It turned out to be fortunate that
we were not qualified to be flight instructors. Instead, we
spent our time on the ground soliciting prospective students and talking them into coming to our school rather
than to that of one of our competitors. We left the actual
instructing to the pilots we hired, who were then on a
one-on-one basis, taking over the students we had re-
cruited.

Plan your work; then work your plan.

You cannot expect to follow a simple formula, designed
to move people from rags to riches. In everything you undertake when setting goals, you must personalize your plan
of action. For example, visualize yourself as having already
achieved your goal. This not only gives you a clearer idea
of what you want to achieve but creates confidence and belief in yourself that you really can achieve the goal. Ideas
are your most valuable asset, without which there can be no
action. When you are looking for a guide to success and are
having difficulty determining what you really want in your
career or working life, do some extensive homework. What
do people want that they are now having trouble getting, in
the way of products or services or consultation? Pinpoint a
need—something simple and within your sphere of experience—and fill it. You will be surprised at the results.

SELF STARTER

Jot down on paper a description of a consumer need
you think is not being supplied by any business in
your area. Given the necessary funding, would you
ever consider launching a business to fill this need?

"No matter what ventures you undertake, place a high priority on sharing with other people," insists Van Andel.

A sound business must be people-oriented. Understanding begins with respect. Only people make things happen. Only individuals drive nails to construct buildings. Only individuals serve as doctors, or run computers, or drive trucks, or teach school, or design bridges, or conduct research. That's how simple it is and that's why a successful company works—because it not only relies on people but respects them as individuals.

As we developed our own business, we found a remarkable thing happening: the more we relied on other people and became sensitive to their needs, the more the enterprise prospered and expanded. We made it a point to try in every way to attract and associate with people whose outlooks were positive and discourage those who were naysayers. Thus, it was easy for us to become other-centered and to deflect praise and recognition that came our way—without seeming to do so—to those who worked with us and for us.

We also learned the importance of timing, at first because we started our present company at a time when the need for our kinds of consumer products and our type of service and our concepts of doing business was beginning to grow. As Shakespeare said, "There's a tide in the affairs of man which, taken at the flood, leads on to fortune. Omitted, the voyage of life is bound to miseries and shallows."

Think about that concept in today's world—almost four centuries later.

We came at the right time to the right place—and with the right people. And we have ever since emphasized to those who work with us that the calendar and the clock are essential instruments to success. We do not mean or imply that you have to be a clock-watcher or set up some kind of bizarre formula based on the theory that Monday is a poor day to plan important discussions or that Wednesdays and Thursdays are the best days to make sales pitches. Rather, we promote the policy of doing business—whatever it is—in such a way that the people who benefit from your products or services or counsel do so at those times that are most convenient and productive for them.

As the old lyric had it, "Your time is my time."

Think of people, regardless of race, color, creed, or economic status, as individuals who share with each other the same basic needs for the esentials of life, love, recognition, hope, communication, and personal freedom from want and oppression. There is still far too much emphasis in today's society on class, status, income, and other artificial concepts. Think of individuals in terms of human energy and the innate potential for accomplishment in some chosen field of endeavor.

You will never regret it if you choose to coordinate your actions and goals with good, hard, productive work. That is the stuff that life is made of.

Two hundred years ago, Thomas Jefferson wrote, "A good leader inspires others with confidence in him; but a great leader inspires them with confidence in themselves."

As we have emphasized, people who would succeed must take action today and not look to tomorrow as a time when it will be easier to achieve something or when the timing will be better or when they will have acquired more experience. But your concept of tomorrow is essential, once you have put your plan in motion and taken action. It is not enough to stand on your present achievements. You must always look forward and move on. Adlai E. Stevenson hit the nail on the head when he advised, "We dare not just look back to great yesterdays. We must look forward to great tomorrows."

Freedom's Choice

Free enterprise is one of the fundamental concepts that has made possible the widespread personal freedom we enjoy in America. Yet we risk being indifferent to the power of freedom because it is something we have inherited. We underestimate its value and we forget what an enormous sacrifice our own forefathers had to make to establish its roots in the nation.

We have the choice of accepting or rejecting challenges great and small and either tackling them in our own way or sitting back and letting someone else do it. Sometimes, of course, we take on too much and have to retrench. "It is like the time we decided to enter a boat race in the open sea, in a region where we had not sailed before," ruefully recalled DeVos, who is now an accomplished sailor, but was then a novice.

Everything went magnificently at first. The sun was out and there was a steady breeze and, though we were up against some much more experienced sailors, we seemed to be holding our position quite well. Then the clouds rolled in and the wind came up.

Before we knew it, we were scudding along in the teeth of what seemed to us to be a major gale. The waves were whipped up and the salt stung our eyes and we had trouble keeping on course. We knew we were licked but we hung on—that is until seasickness began taking its course and half of us wished we would be swept overboard and die rather than remain in such agony. To make a long story short, we gave up the race and headed back for port.

As we approached the dock, battered and the worse for wear, we were greeted with some disdain by an old salt who helped us tie up the boat. He was not at all convinced when one of our crew said that we would still be out there fighting if only there had been a cure for seasickness.

"Is that so?" he laughed. "Well, I have a sure cure for seasickness."

"What's that?" we asked in one breath.

"Go sit under a tree."

Fortunately, the free-enterprise system lets some people sit under trees while others get into the action. But this has not always been so. We were surprised to be told by a history buff recently that more than half of all the activity on behalf of free enterprise, for example, has taken place in the United States, and most of that within the past century. Those facts alone are statistics that should inspire us to participate in the promotion of free enterprise and spread its significance and implications to others.

One of the most impressive qualities of freedom is that it can function to the benefit of people whose very ideas and goals are contrary to each other, or in direct competition. The Democrats enjoy freedom; but so do the Republicans. General Motors enjoys freedom; but so does Ford. The producers of coal and oil enjoy freedom; but so do the environmentalists who oppose them.

Going back to the sailing story and also the earlier mention of the "Four Winds" speech, it is pertinent to liken freedom to the four winds. The figure of speech is applicable. No matter which way the winds are blowing and no matter which way you have to go to reach your goal, you can learn how to use the winds to advantage. If you know your goal, you will not let an opposing wind prevent you from reaching it. You simply take a different course to get there, tacking back and forth in a manner that, surprisingly, lets you utilize contradictory winds to make headway.

The moral of this little story is that, if you are inspired to reach a certain objective, you will actually find ways to use an opposing force to reach it.

SELF STARTER

Bring to mind the name of someone in your community who reached a noteworthy goal despite an opposing "wind." How did he or she achieve this objective?

Man's Material Welfare

Like the winds, other natural resources play a vital role in helping would-be achievers along the road to success. Man's material welfare can actually be visualized in a formula used occasionally by DeVos and Van Andel that looks like this:

$$MMW = NR + HE \times T$$

Translated, this means that Man's Material Welfare is the product of Natural Resources plus Human Energy, multiplied by Tools.

The cornerstone of a free society is a man's right to use his own tools, the essential connection between economics and freedom in a system of free enterprise. This system is in direct contrast to Russia, which is forty years behind the United States economically and which, despite its claim to being a land of farmers and farmlands, is agriculturally poor and even has to turn to America to obtain enough grain to feed its population.

We spend a lot of time prattling with words and too little time defining just what freedom is in contrast to what the Communist system is. But it should be made clear that the development of methods for improving peoples' material welfare in no way implies that we downplay those intangible qualities that are so vital to success—qualities like inspiration and spiritualism and faith.

Inspiration is essential. But once we are inspired to set our goals, then we have to commit ourselves to the real work that is required to achieve what we have in mind. That is why tools are such a vital part of the MMW formula. Our output is multiplied in direct relationship to the use of tools. Compare what we produce in America, for example, with what is produced in countries like India or Peru, where there is a great lack of tools and where the standard of living is so abysmal as to brook no comparison at all with our own.

Compare our motivational system, too, with that of China and other Communist nations. The great differential here is that in America the people own the tools, whereas in Communist countries the tools are the property of the state and there is no incentive to use them wisely or care for them properly. Every time a government takes over the tools and thus negates the users' pride of ownership and accomplishment, productivity takes a step backward.

The message here is that we must choose our goals and alternatives well in advance and not sit back and wait until a crisis occurs or it is too late to take any effective action. As Benjamin Franklin said in his usual succinct way, "When the well is dry, we know the wealth of water."

CHAPTER
6

Choices Versus Responsibilities

"If choice is real, if there really are alternatives, it follows that, in choosing between them, we are exhibiting our power as real agents, real causes and initiators of new departures in the flow of cosmic change."

—F.C.S. Von Schiller

How many people do you know who feel that their lives are constantly controlled by circumstances? Most people feel this way, to greater or lesser degrees. Yet they are living under a misapprehension. Almost everyone we have ever met has the opportunities and options to make choices. People tend to feel that they are powerless and cannot make meaningful choices. They have too many children. Or too little money. Or a lack of education. Or the competition is too tough. One thing or another is always against them. They become afraid to try. So they simply give up.

We mentioned earlier that, despite the prevalence of this attitude, all of us in our present system of American society have three vital assets:

- The *power* to choose
- The *ability* to choose
- The *right* to choose

Start by evaluating your own outlook on the subject. Do you have a "fix-it" mentality and make plans for dealing with a problem? Or do you have a "woe is me" outlook, complaining that the cards are stacked against you and you have no choices in the matter?

Those are the two basic ways that people approach this question of choice and dealing with life.

"People often ask us," says DeVos,

What do you do when you really do *not* have any choice—when something is inevitable, when a person

107

dies, when there is nothing you can do to change an eventual result?

The answer is that you always have the choice of what attitude you take, which can, in effect, change the impact that the "inevitable" may have on your life and well-being.

There are two other ways to look at the subject of choice: (1) What do you do with failure? (2) What do you do with success? The two hardest things in life to deal with are at the opposite ends of the pole: success and failure. Which one would you choose? Well, you do have a choice! And your choice is likely to affect the future as well as the present since success breeds success and failure begets failure.

In our own business, it so happens that we offer this kind of choice to people at many age levels and from various walks of society. And some have had dismal failures and some have been unbelievably successful. Another question has been asked us from time to time: Are people always aware that they had failures because they made bad choices?

The answer varies. Sometimes not for years afterwards. And sometimes never. Many people go through life and are never conscious of making choices. They go about daily lives like everyone else they know. They see the same people, go to the same places, eat the same kinds of meals, hold the same kinds of jobs. Things all seemed to happen without any evidence of choice-making.

What they do not realize—and what we sometimes have trouble getting across to people—is that every single day, every hour, you are making choices of one kind or another. Although some are important and some minimal, they are all *choices*. Eventually these choices—even seemingly insignificant ones—lead people down one road or another. Life propels you onward unless you just roll over and give up. These are all options.

Celebrate Choice Day

Unlike most commemorative events, every day in your life is a *choice* day. There are no big announcements from heaven as to what is the right choice and what is the wrong one in each instance—that is up to the individual. Yet the power of choice is a God-given attribute.

Some choices lead to much more significant things than the opposite choice might have resulted in. What really are the consequences of having made a decision and gone in one direction instead of another? You can look back on your life and surely come up with examples. Think about Rich and Jay and that choice they made years ago that was seemingly insignificant: to share a car in order to go to school every day instead of traveling separately. That was a seemingly simple choice, a mere matter of convenience, but it led to their becoming fast friends and that, in turn, led to joint business ventures and eventually enormous changes in their lives.

Some things you do or don't do hang over your life like a wet blanket forever. This is true, say, of young people who decide whether to continue their education or not, to head for a certain career or not, to get married or stay single, to have children or be childless. Yet, rather than taking the initiative, many young people put off decisions altogether and grouse about the problems their generation faces. We are here to tell you that, when it comes to such problems, there is nothing new under the sun. Generations upon generations have had similar problems going back to the times of the cave people.

Are you worried sick sometimes that you have made—or might make—the wrong choice? Well, believe us, you are in good company when it comes to trying to anticipate the future correctly. Consider these gems of foggy forecasting:

- Back in the second century, the great Greek astronomer, Ptolemy, stated that it was clear that the earth was in the middle of the universe.
- In 1899, the commissioner of the United States Office of Patents proclaimed that everything that could be invented had by then already been invented.

- Harry Warner, who started Warner Pictures in 1927 said, "Who in the world wants to hear actors talk? All we need is silent films."
- President Grover Cleveland once proclaimed, "Sensible and responsible women do not want to vote."
- Robert Milliken, a great scientist who won the Nobel prize in 1923, said, "There is no likelihood that man can ever tap the power of the atom."
- Lord Kelvin, president of the Royal Society of Science in 1895, said, "Heavier-than-air flying machines are impossible."
- And in 1929, just before the stock market crash, the United States Department of Labor predicted that 1930 would be "a splendid employment year"!

Every age has to endure its share of bonehead predictions and humbug expertise. For every successful leader there are a dozen would-be "authorities" who claim falsely to have the inside track on truth and consequences.

We have discovered that anyone who dares to choose excellence as a goal and dares to dream big, risks hearing self-satisfied snickers and dire predictions from the dour crowd on the sidelines. That's because many people find it easy to criticize what they do not understand, cannot comprehend, or are unwilling to accept.

When opportunities come your way, you have a choice: to take them or leave them. That is the very moment when you must decide: "Do I pack up and forget the future? Or do I turn a deaf ear to the doomsayers and decide to do what needs to be done to succeed?"

Winners make that decision instinctively. They make the choice and move forward, knowing full well that the only persons who can control their destinies are themselves.

Well, we don't believe the naysayers and the prophets of doom. But we do believe in the art of the possible. And we believe that, together, we can fly to unimaginable heights, and will achieve the "impossible."

The Quality of Excellence

People think in terms of excellence, including success, wealth, achievements, and gracious living. We feel uncomfortable about things at the lower end of the scale. We become anxious about peoples and nations in the grip of poverty. It makes us uneasy and often guilty to think of starving children and then realize what bounties we have in America. Yet we should always bear in mind that poor people cannot help other poor people. What we can do, however, is to condition ourselves to speak out and stand up for those things in which we believe. To do this effectively, we must first have faith—faith in self, faith in God, faith in our convictions. Once these conditions are met, you will be amazed at how easy it is to speak out.

Success usually requires sacrifice. You have to give up certain pleasures in order to devote time and effort to goals with higher priorities. Are you ready now?

SELF STARTER

List two goals you would like to attain that require substantial sacrifices. What are these sacrifices and why are they hindering your attempts at achievement?

Some form of sacrifice exists in respect to almost everything of any consequence that people want to achieve. We have stated in a number of different ways that success breeds success. This assertion is based on the proven fact that people who are successful continue to be so because they realize that they can be successful, and because they have to give up something—time, pleasure, a trip, a sport—in order to attain some of their ends. With this in mind, contemplate how really great you can be and how much power you have in you—the power to make things happen. Once you strike that attitude, you will never stop or let up.

Despite the attention paid to excellence, the quality of excellence may really be cn the decline. Why? Largely because people lack the faith that they can rise above mediocrity. In our society, power blocks have developed in which multitudes of people are trying to do the least and get the most for as little action as possible and with minimal effort.

We have to counter this by understanding how we can do more in order to get more, how we can escalate a faith in ourselves and a belief in our own worth to attain much higher goals in life. By doing so, we restore the whole concept of America and how it was developed through a striving for excellence on the part of our forefathers.

There is a strange and inexplicable trend today to apologize for success and to proclaim poverty and nonachievement as virtues. Being low key is the *in* thing these days, even if it seems to be nothing more than doing nothing.

Are you going to settle for mediocrity or strive for excellence? The choice is yours. Do you want to achieve things or simply line up a few percs, such as minimal expenses for entertaining or the use of a personal car?

Many people equate success in terms of status, preferring to be the captain of a small ship rather than one of many officers on an ocean liner. They feel—although it is not always true—that they will get more recognition on the one hand and avoid much of the tediousness on the other hand. Linking yourself to community provides this ''small ship'' atmosphere because, even though the community is an urban one or quite large, the people who volunteer are likely to hold informal, even amateur, standings.

Working in community, you are also likely to encounter a good many people who are older, looking for a purpose in life, or lonely. As we said earlier, if you want to move a lot of people in a certain direction, locate the lonely individuals of this world and offer them something that will counteract their isolation. Most people have certain feelings of loneliness, even if they are relatively secure in a family or group. This sometimes translates into a feeling that they lack some kind of recognition they had hoped for—rather than simply being physically isolated from other people. So one form of motivation is the need to combat this void in peoples' lives.

King of the Hill

Many of our friends, recounting childhood days, recall a game we used to play called king of the hill. It was kind of a disorganized, push-and-pull activity in which each youthful player attempted to get to the top of the designated hill, whether it was a mound of earth, a large packing crate, or a participant's front porch. The eventual victor was the one who could knock down, push away, or outjump all the other kids and proclaim himself king.

We know of a lot of people long past childhood who are still playing king of the hill, trying to get to the top by knocking off their competitors. Some of these latter-day monarchs have been ruthless in the way they have cut down the competition, leading us to wonder again and again why so many people think it necessary to be the lone victor in order to achieve success in their field.

We wish that some of them could have been with us when we visited the site of the ancient city of Ephesus. There, a succession of kings ruled this part of Asia Minor, each in turn conquering all contenders in order to stand alone at the top, inevitably for only brief periods of time and constantly fearful of being toppled by someone stronger. Where is the glory now, buried in the ruins of the Temple of Diana?

Although this kind of pushiness is to be disparaged, it is somewhat less injurious to the individual than manipulation. We all know people who, failing to get what they want in any other way, will try all kinds of manipulative maneuvers to achieve their ends. They may bring pressure to bear on other people or resort to what politicians on Capitol Hill refer to as ''dirty tricks.'' These are subtle tactics used to get people under one's thumb through various subterfuges, such as playing on their feelings of guilt, voicing disapproval, using flattery to distort their judgment, making them feel insecure, or implying that their behavior is strange or different from that of normal people. Experienced, calculating manipulators know the vulnerabilities of individuals and exploit that knowledge to arouse a person's emotions and create internal pressure. As a result, those who are manipulated tend to lose their objectivity and then feel used.

You can avoid falling into the manipulation trap by recognizing the procedures that are being used and by trying to evaluate the reasons why you are the target and intended victim.

SELF STARTER

Have you been manipulated in this manner recently? If so, how did it happen, what did you do to counteract the action, and what was the result?

Those who are experts at manipulating are often very adept at criticism, a form of ammunition that is effective in forcing people to do their will. This does not mean, however, that you should be suspicious of or ignore all criticism as an evil. Some of it may be meaningful and relevant. What you have to do is to accept the fact that some criticism can be positive and constructive. Treat it for what it is worth and act accordingly.

We all know individuals who not only accept criticism constructively but actually invite it in order to improve themselves. People who react well to criticism and take corrective action will first evaluate the source of the criticism. They pay little attention to the naysayers who make something of a hobby of panning institutions and putting people down. But they listen carefully if the criticism comes from a person whose role is objective and whose qualifications are both valid and acceptable.

Those who respond well to criticism do not take offense and try some form of counterattack. We are all human and it is human nature when someone informs us that we have done something distasteful to react with a "look who's talking!" attitude. People who can accept criticism gracefully also strive to communicate if they doubt the validity of the criticism, rather than retreating into silence. Thus, it is important to have nurtured the talent for dialogue that we talked about earlier.

Rich and Jay comment that they encounter or see criticism all the time in the business of selling. People are taken to task for using the wrong sales approach, not being aggressive enough, failing to meet a reasonable quota, or not having done their homework about a new product. The salespeople who become successful are the ones who can sit back and evaluate the criticism, reject assumptions that are out of line, and take to heart those comments that are valid.

Finally, they moderate any feelings of antagonism or indignation they may have initially and try to understand their critics. At the very least, this sometimes leads a critic to retract a comment that was too outspoken or explain what was meant that may have sounded too negative.

What it all boils down to in the end is that we have to live together with other people, not all of whom will see eye to eye with each other. Individuals can, of course, choose to live alone in the wilderness and thus avoid having to conform to the lifestyles of others.

Again, we have the choice. We are not forced. But we must understand the nature of this community that we are either accepting or rejecting.

Community and Accountability

If people are held accountable, they must also be free to make their own choices. Accountability and freedom go hand in hand. Accountability must always include evaluation. If people are to be held accountable, then it is necessary that their performances be evaluated and susceptible to judgment and the resulting rewards or penalties. People reap what they sow, and this must be taught in schools, at home, on the job, and in all walks of life.

Communities, despite the appearance of substantiality they many reflect, are fragile and sometimes tenuous bodies at best, subject to disintegration and change. Like institutions, even including some of the most established churches, they tend to go through a four-stage cycle over the years. The first stage is the one labeled *building,* when plans are activated, public works are established, and many dedicated people serve long and hard to achieve common goals.

The second stage is that of *management,* when leaders of the community (or any other body or institution) learn how to manage and administer. Although the term has the connotation of being productive, this is actually a downtrend because those who were builders now become so busy managing that they no longer are building. This is the stage at which politics enters the picture, not always for the best.

The third stage, in addition to being a downtrend, is a negative one and might best be referred to as *defensive.* Now the builders who have slipped down into the role of managers are endlessly involved in forming excuses for their failure to keep on building and growing.

The last stage is that of *blaming.* This is the era of finger-pointing, shifting the blame for the failure to keep on building. It is the same old story that we hear day in and day out on Capitol Hill in which congress blames the president for failures and the president blames congress.

It's time we got back to being *builders!*

By this time, everyone has finally realized that there is something wrong and there is even a chance that, with proper leadership, the community can revive itself and get back to stage number one.

The Fear of Success

People—and there are many—moan and groan that there is little difference between Communism and Capitalism because you are slaves in both cases, whether to a system or to corporate managers. But they lose sight of the accomplishments of generations of free Americans who are, and have been, anything but slaves.

These critics also reflect a curious but common ailment: the *fear of success,* a distrust of those in leadership roles. This fear has existed for centuries, long before the birth of America. A Greek orator, Isocrates, said in 430 B.C., "One must now apologize for any success in business as though it were a violation of the moral law, so that today it is worse to prosper than to be a criminal!"

This kind of situation is indeed ironic when we consider how many millions of immigrants have reached American shores with the express idea of trying to resurrect their lives and their ambitions. The "boat people," seeking asylum in the United States from places like Cuba and Haiti and Asia are nothing new. The first "boat people" to arrive on this continent landed on the shores of what is now Jamestown, Virginia, in 1607. Others stepped ashore at Plymouth in 1620—and the boats have been coming ever since.

Those who fear success are often the most outspoken in denouncing people who are successful or institutions that thrive. They like to cry "Capitalism!" and paint America as a land where wealthy corporate bosses and the barons of Wall Street dictate our careers, culture, and even the way we dress. They deliberately overlook the fact that small business is the heart of the American history of achievement, which among other things has created more than 90 percent of all the new, nongovernment jobs in the last decade.

Those who fear success often erroneously associate it with bigness. Yet America is a real land of opportunity for small ventures. You can make a living from nine to five, five days a week in the corporate world. But you make a success during those other hours and days when the rest of the world is coasting. You are free to do whatever you want, but if you want to get ahead, then you have to have the personal discipline to tackle some of the chores you do not really want to do.

This kind of freedom to choose one's course of action and application to work is one of the fundamentals of the free enterprise system. But freedom is a tender plant—rare, hard to start, difficult to cultivate, fragile, and constantly in need of attention. Greed and force destroy it. Like clean air, it is hardly noticed until suddenly one day it is gone. You have to continue to work for personal freedom and not put things off until the well is dry or a drought has spread over the land.

SELF STARTER

What is your most precious personal freedom? Is there any danger that you might lose it? If so, why?

The Price of Personal Choice

Although freedom implies the strong element of personal choice, it does not come without paying a price. There is no such thing as a free lunch. When someone gets something for nothing, then someone else gets nothing for something.

To get ahead and make achievements, you need more than robust good intentions. You need to act, to have goals, to relate to the people who are accomplishing things themselves. In this you have full freedom—to succeed or fail. The first criterion for success in a business—any business—is to have a strong desire to be successful.

Not everyone is eager enough to succeed to pay the price that is exacted for success. And not a few people look upon success as something that will imbue them with feelings of guilt. That is one of the most important reasons why you should ally yourself with a concept, like the free enterprise system itself, which has become recognized as a beneficial as well as a motivating force in which its participants can take pride.

Success is not sinful. Despite the overabundance of hungry and poverty-stricken people in the world, we need not feel guilty because we have achieved material success and can enjoy full stomachs. You will never lift up others by lowering yourself. It is a tragic misconception that we must all settle for mediocrity and hide behind the comforting shield of being average, instead of striving for excellence and greater levels of achievement.

Your own front door may be your most serious roadblock in seeking success. You have to *go out of it* first, when it is admittedly much easier and you are less vulnerable to confrontation if you stay inside and avoid worrying about all the problems and misfits and dangers that lie beyond.

Most businesspeople today are honest and fair. Those who operate on the basis of greed and manipulation, in fact, are not likely to be successful and in the end are done in, one way or another, by their own dishonesty and scheming.

"To become successful," said a man who had started with almost nothing and become a top sales executive, "you need to acquaint yourself with success." The key word there is *acquaint*. You cannot be successful if you do not first understand what success is, especially in regard to your own aspirations and hopes. We are creatures of God, placed on earth for a reason and created as individuals in His light. The Creator did not intend us to be drudges, slaving from dawn to dusk just to earn a living. He presents His own image in many forms so that we can recognize greatness when we see it and when we have a chance to emulate it.

The Choices of Freedom

Nothing inspires people with such great impact as the realization that a certain course of action will bring them one or more freedoms, including the freedom to make the best of their opportunities on the one hand and freedom from want and oppression on the other hand. But freedom does exact a price. It is something you can have for yourself only when you are willing to share it with other people. We must always be careful how we exercise freedom so that we do not deny it to others and so that we make it more possible for others to enjoy it.

Give a hand, not a handout. People want your help and your understanding, but they do not want charity. They also want a real sense of involvement. When you work with other people who may not have much of a say in whatever enterprise you are engaged in, you will succeed much better if you will make them feel *involved,* that they are wanted and that their voices and their labors are needed to make things work out right. *Recognition* is one of the most crucial—and often the easiest—of the many contributions you can make to progress. We know full well, from past experience, that no one ever likes to be left out, to be unsung. When you have the opportunity to make a choice, to grant recognition or to ignore it, always opt for the former. It will pay off.

People who are creative are particularly susceptible to recognition, if not praise. Often they are engaged in work assignments whose results are not readily apparent. If you hire a person to mow your lawn, or to build a bookcase, you can see quickly how well the job is done. But if you commission an artist to make sketches or a writer to compose verses, the quality of the work is likely to be limited to the eyes and opinions of the beholders. So recognition and praise are the only means the artist or the writer may have to judge whether the creative attempt has succeeded or failed.

Inspiration, whether originating from within or from exterior forces, is the catalyst that makes us determined to improve the quality of our lives. As the noted church leader and author, Robert Schuller, expressed it, ''The qualities of peoples' lives are in direct proportion to their commitment to excellence.''

The Six Faiths

Picture a series of concentric circles like a paper target on a rifle range, each circle getting smaller and focusing in on the target at the center, which is labeled *YOU*. The concept here is to enlarge your horizons and your personal strength by taking advantage of broader existing strengths and having faith in each of them individually and all of them collectively.

Ranging from the outer circle to the innermost, there are six basic faiths you can choose, among others, to help build your inner strength. These are:

1. *Faith in Faith.* You gain strength through belief in God, a higher power, no matter which religion you select to support you.
2. *Faith in America.* The strongest nation in the world can impart its own power directly to you if you will only identify strongly as a believer in your country.
3. *Faith in Free Enterprise.* Identify with the system that has, since the nation's founding, been the key to success and happiness for Americans in varied enterprises and all fields of work.
4. *Faith in Community.* Whether you live in a tiny rural village or a great metropolis, identify with the community in which you and your family live. You don't have to be a tireless volunteer or an avid do-gooder—simply establish your roots and you'll thrive.
5. *Faith in Family.* Whether you belong to a large family or simply have a handful of relatives, take pride in your heritage.
6. *Faith in Yourself.* Lastly, and most importantly, believe in yourself and what you can accomplish.

CHAPTER
7

Choices in the Marketplace

"When making a choice in life, self-respect is a wonderful thing, so long as it is not motivated by self-deception."

—Billy Graham

There has been a disturbing trend in recent years that relates to the concept of work, especially among young people who have become strongly career-oriented and who want to make a name for themselves in their profession or field of endeavor. This pattern increasingly tends to separate the career, on the one hand, and the home, on the other. Partly this has occurred because of natural forces and situations as more and more people have commuted some distance to their places of work, thus enforcing a geographical, as well as a chronological schism.

While it is often relaxing, if not refreshing, to be able to remove oneself from the work environment before nine and after five and on weekends, a certain deterioration occurs that is not often immediately detectable. The work environment suffers from a lack of the kind of moral tone that exists in the household and in the community. This could well be the reason why the country has been concerned about ethics—both personal and corporate—and the shocking discovery that seemingly ''nice'' and often family-oriented men and women have become embroiled in shady deals, if not outright crimes, in order to try to make more money.

It is vital for people whose jobs take them outside their hometowns to try to develop a stronger understanding of home and community ethics and keep them in mind when they are at work, as well as when they are with their own families.

Voluntarism

Do you have inclinations to become an integral part of a larger congregation?

One of the most difficult choices for many people to make is often that of becoming part of the community and learning how to draw strength through the roots that have been established. This is most frequently the case with people whose jobs and careers and activities take them out of their communities for a large percentage of the time. The term *bedroom community* has become commonplace, referring to those suburbs that are within an easy commute to places of work and many of whose occupants are little involved in local affairs.

On the same side of the coin is the metropolis, where people dwell for years without ever trying to establish roots because the environment around them is too immense and too heavily populated.

People say they choose small towns because they are friendlier. But remember—as this book emphasized before—that a city is not a *thing*. It is made up of people, each one involved with problems and aspirations and challenges that are similar to those of the people who live in towns and villages. Those who choose to help their neighborhoods are likely to be better citizens, but equally importantly, they derive more pleasure from their lives and their work.

The advantage in deciding to link yourself strongly to a community is that you can enhance your stature and draw strength from others without restricting yourself. In our American society, you have the freedom to be very independent or to position yourself in a well structured environment where you function between narrow parameters. Some people need a certain restrictiveness in order to succeed, whether in a career, in society, in marriage, or any other aspect of human life.

Nobody is truly independent in the larger sense of the word. Our choices are all subject to limitations, even though these strictures may come from our inner selves as much as from outward forces. If you fail to recognize these restrictions and limitations, the chances are that you will fail in your goals. If you elect to volunteer for community service for the public good, take enough time to assess your capabilities and understand how you can best meet the needs at hand. What you like to do may often be at variance with what you really can do.

Many people actually do not know how to get involved to begin with, much less put their talents to good use when they find themselves accepted as a volunteer.

The democratic system itself is based on voluntarism, requiring that a great many citizens give willingly and generously of their time in order to help improve society. Those who refuse to get involved in politics will live to regret the fact that they will be continuously at the mercy of those who do. The failure to get involved in your community functions will in the same way leave you at the mercy of those who do participate. The volunteers eventually become the ones who make the decisions, set the standards, write the rules, and guide the lifestyles of the community. You simply have to become involved in order to protect your territory, your ideas, and your preferences. The danger in not participating is that you will have little or no say in what your community is going to be like, for better or worse.

In a sense, we all have to pay for the space we occupy on this planet in one way or another. We "pay rent" to our town and state and country, to assist in matters relating to faith, government, and political procedures. We have to assume that responsibility by getting involved. But the majority of people do not volunteer well. Few know what to volunteer for, how to get involved, and how best to utilize the talents and experience they may have. It all revolves around a sense of responsibility. But it must be an intelligent and productive involvement, as well as the realization that one's help is needed.

There are far too many citizens who do not have this sense of responsibility at all. They say, "Let the other guy do it," or "I'm too harassed . . . too busy . . . too important." The excuses are many. People who donate money often do not think that they ought to give any time and people who give time sometimes do so in lieu of giving money. The giving of the money is just as important as the giving of time. We often hear the complaint, "But you only gave money and I devoted a lot of time. . . ."

The answer is that money is time. Some dignity should be given to each, since one is just as important as the other. People are always trying to find out how much someone else gave before they make a financial commitment, but that is not our business. Our goal should be to give money, time, and talent to the causes closest to our heart and stop worrying about what the other people are doing.

"We held a meeting recently on participation," commented Jay Van Andel,

and talked about the dozens of projects we all had worked for individually or jointly over the past decade. When the subject of donations came up, we asked, "Are any of you feeling poorer because of past contributions?" The answer was negative. In fact, those who made substantial donations replied that they actually felt richer because the community as a whole had been enhanced and improved.

It is a great challenge to be a life enricher. The late Walt Disney used to say that there were three kinds of people in town: (1) well poisoners, who were always dumping water on other peoples' parades, (2) lawn mowers, who kept their lawns trim but never volunteered to cut the neighbors' grass or do anything outside their own property, and (3) the life enrichers who went out of their way to help others.

If our goal is to enrich the lives of others then our lives in turn will become richer. If we help them to achieve, then we too become achievers.

The Essence and Spirit of Voluntarism

As Rich DeVos and Jay Van Andel pointed out recently when preparing a series of public service ads on voluntarism, "We know hundreds of folks who have devoted much of their time and work to volunteer programs." Here are thumbnail biographies of just a few whom they have cited and whose efforts have been particularly unique and meaningful.

Carl Wallace founded Wish Upon A Star in his hometown of Evansville, Indiana, to aid youthful patients who have malignant or life-threatening illnesses. Through his organization, seriously ill children are taken on trips— oftentimes their last—to fulfill their wishes to visit certain places or participate in events they have long desired to experience.

Ruth Hardwick, a former nurse in her seventies, used her monthly checks from Social Security to open the Charity Restaurant in Perth Amboy, New Jersey. Seven days a week, three times a day, she began feeding the area's homeless people. After her daughter died tragically at the age of forty-four, Mrs. Hardwick took the $50,000 she received from her daughter's life insurance policy and added that to funds to feed the hungry.

Fred White, a Chicago Park District program director, launched a program called Plastic on Parks to collect discarded plastic containers and turn them into building materials to rebuild the city's aging playgrounds. Melted down and molded into planks, the plastic logs formed playground walls and seating areas for more than 330 playgrounds over a three-year period. In addition, the program developed by White and his corps of volunteers has gone a long way toward recycling waste and protecting the environment.

Esther Wolf left her consulting business to become the administrator of a Kansas City health clinic so decrepit it was on the verge of being closed. Working long hours and with the help of other volunteers, she transformed the Richard Cabot Clinic into an institution that provides medical care to poor Hispanic families. Along the way, she has also helped other minority groups and established sites where senior citizens can gather daily for meals and social services.

Ronald Post, president and founder of Northwest Medical Teams in Salem, Oregon, saw his opportunity for a unique kind of service when he stared aghast at a telecast of Cambodian children dying from starvation in

Thailand. Swinging into action, he organized a volunteer medical team and within two weeks he and his associates were in Southeast Asia working day and night. Since then, Post and his volunteers have helped alleviate famine in Ethiopia, aided victims of an earthquake in El Salvador, and treated lip and palate deformities that were ravaging Mexican Indians in the villages of Oaxaca.

Donnalee Velvick, motivated by her own experiences as an abused, often homeless child who lived in railroad yards and foster homes, has dedicated her life to children whose lives have been similarly affected. She founded Hope House in the countryside south of Nampa, Idaho, where as many as forty-two children have been sheltered. This resourceful and energetic lady runs the operation effectively on a shoestring, soliciting grants from businesses and individuals and often barters products they make (such as canned fruits) to take the youngsters on overnight trips and recreational jaunts.

Consuello Harper, a sharecropper's daughter, first saw her calling when she stood outside a pool hall in the rain in one of the toughest neighborhoods of Montgomery, Alabama, and tried to convince winos, prostitutes, and pimps that they could become somebody if they really wanted to. A few responded to her message and she eventually secured enough funds to establish an Opportunity Industrial Training Center, which has helped more than 6,000 of the down-and-out find a way up.

Putting Yourself to the Test

Surprisingly, you may have aptitudes that you are not aware of and that can be strengthened through experience with community service. People who do not like to sell products or services, for example, may often be better at selling than those who are naturals or claim they enjoy it. Why? Because they conscientiously apply themselves more to the job.

Rich and Jay are firm believers in this phenomenon, having attended hundreds of testimonial events for people who have set records in selling who had never been trained in sales, never served as professional salespersons, and had no intentions originally of ever making a career in selling. A characteristic example is that of a lady we'll call Maude in Des Moines, Iowa, who sold 35 percent more products in one year than the runner-up, a man who had been in sales for two decades. Yet she had been in the business less than three years, signing up after retiring as a schoolteacher where her major "selling" efforts were directed at keeping pupils motivated.

How did she manage this miracle?

"I don't sell anything at all," she explains. "I show people products I use and believe in and tell them how lucky I've been to find food supplements and household cleaners that live up to their claims and are reasonable in cost, and safe to the environment. Then my prospective customers sell themselves and buy. The very best way to sell anything—products, services, even yourself—is to offer people a chance to make their own choice."

This same principle is true in the field of voluntarism we have just discussed. For the most part, these volunteers became involved in areas that they previously had known little about. They were successful because they immersed themselves fully in something they believed in and there was no doubt in anyone's mind that they believed in what they were doing and practiced what they preached.

Choosing community projects may be just what you need to determine how well you can seize opportunities and show the way. No matter what field you are in, you can take a leadership role in doing something that may never have been done before. Leadership is made up of a lot of little things, such as making choices, keeping an open mind, welcoming the ideas of others, sensing when others are either uncomfortable or at ease, giving credit where it is due, reconciling opposing factions, being aware of trends, being able to compromise realistically without sacrificing moral principles, giving recognition to contributions made by various people, initiating change, inspiring follow-through from associates, being trusted to keep confidences, and above all having faith.

One of the benefits of community association and public service stems from the fact that you have to analyze situations that exist and then choose the role that you intend to play.

Expressing who and what you are and making decisions about where you stand helps you to clarify your concept of yourself.

The Nine-to-Five Syndrome

Time and time again, we hear people complain, ''I've been working too hard and am dead tired.'' Some people have the notion that if they start working before nine in the morning or continue working after five in the afternoon, they should just naturally be fatigued. But the truth of the matter is quite different. The people we know who have the most energy and almost never seem to be tired are the ones who work long hours and who think nothing of getting up early to tackle a job or using the evening hours for productive activities. Why should this be so?

One answer is that the people with seemingly boundless energy are exhilarated by work. They enjoy what they have chosen to do in life and they find that activity invigorates body and spirit like a tonic. This is evident in our own business where people absolutely have to function outside the confines of the traditional nine-to-five routine. The ones who are the most successful consistently devote long hours to their work. Not only that, but they usually are working hand in hand with spouses and sometimes other members of the family who are engaged in the same programs. The plain fact of the matter is that they like what they are doing and are no more tired by work than they are by the enjoyment of a favorite hobby.

You can make a living from nine to five, but you make a *success* during those other hours and days when most of the rest of the workforce is coasting. You are free to do those things you want to do, but you must have personal discipline to do some of the things you don't want to do, in order to get ahead.

If, on the one hand, you have chosen the wrong field of endeavor, the chances are that you will find your work boring and frustrating. Boredom and frustration both invite fatigue. If, however, you have chosen a job that is compatible with your interests and your personality, you will find that work consistently buoys you up.

Fortunately, not everyone likes the same field of work. What is manna to one person is indigestible to another. In the end, only you can determine which kind of career will bring you satisfaction and which will drain your energies.

SELF STARTER

List two types of careers you would hate to be in, but which have been voluntarily chosen by two people you know. Why do these people enjoy work you would dislike?

Preventive Prescription for a Healthy Career

In their experiences over the years, Rich and Jay have naturally encountered situations that were disappointing or aggravating. They are the first to admit there is no perfect job in this world and no way of avoiding a certain number of headaches. But their solution—their "preventive medicine," if you will—is to look beyond the frustrations and derive strength and encouragement from the satisfactions that will inevitably come to pass. Among the most important qualities you need to stay on top are:

- Good physical health
- Sound mental health
- Inner spiritual awareness
- A sense of humor

There are, of course, many other qualities that will serve you well. But if you start with the above four, the other essentials will fall in line because you will be a well balanced person. Not everyone can be blessed with brimming good health. A medical study indicates that only about 20 percent of the people who visit their doctors to complain about persistent fatigue actually do have physical or mental ailments lying at the root of the problem. Of this number, more than half can be cured or corrected. So what it boils down to is that only about one person in ten has little or no choice in the matter.

We have met any number of leaders whose workloads were

such that it would have exhausted most people just to hear about them. In some cases, these leaders have been men or women with serious physical defects—the kind that provide marvelous excuses for anyone who wants to get out of work or commitments. Yet they have been so stimulated by their jobs and the challenges they face that they consider their work to be heady and stimulating, and they are often described as having boundless energy.

When Wrong Choices Pay Off

Many people who work hard and are conscientious about the hours they keep and the goals they set are constantly worried that they will make the wrong choices and go in the wrong direction if they are not careful. "How do I know when I am making the right choice?" they ask themselves.

Jay's answer to that question is that this is a needless worry. Every successful person he has ever talked to has made many wrong choices in his or her career. Not only that, but making the wrong choice is oftentimes a blessing in disguise. For one thing, if you have any kind of memory, you will learn not to do that again. Experience tells us what not to do as well as what we ought to do.

Quite a few people worry about making wrong choices for a very personal reason: they think they are losing face. That's nonsense! Tom LaSorda, the baseball manager, has a saying that when things go wrong and you have problems and you wonder what people are thinking, 80 percent of the people who hear about you and your troubles don't care, and the other 20 percent are glad you're having them!

It's all in your attitude. Or, as another popular manager, Yogi Berra said in his own familiar manner, "Attitude is 90 percent. Work is the other half."

A lot of people make negative choices by trying to run away from problems geographically. They don't realize, when they go off to the Caribbean or some other gentle climate, that they are still carrying their problems in their head. The world is not sitting there looking at you. The Caribbean is filled with runaways from reality.

We can draw some comfort from the fact that there are

lousy choices at all levels and positions of society. Our major decision makers, such as the president of the United States and members of congress, make the wrong choices again and again. Some are major blunders that are apparent almost immediately. Some are not apparent for years to come. We used to say during World War II (and probably during all other wars in American history) that the only reason we beat our enemies in battle on numerous occasions was that they made more poor choices than we did!

The worst choice of all is to make no choice. In this case, someone else will make the choice for you and it may be more to your detriment than your making a poor choice. You pay a high price for abdicating your right to make a choice. Many people get hung up because they think that a certain time marks the only occasion in which they can make a certain choice, and that it is unique and earth-shaking. But there is no such thing as the first time this kind of choice has ever been made in the history of the world. Look around, keep your ears and eyes open, and you will have some guidance.

People procrastinate in making choices because they keep waiting for the right advice or the most propitious factors. They overlook the realistic fact that they will never have it all together. There will always be unknowns that have to be accepted. So people sit around waiting for enlightenment that will never come.

We met a man one day who told us his pathetic little story about waiting to make the right choice. His wife had just died and when he was removing some of her clothes from a chest of drawers to give to the undertaker, he came across some expensive lingerie that she had bought on a trip to New York eight or nine years earlier. She was saving it for a special day, which never came.

"I guess this is the special day," said the widower ruefully as he prepared for the funeral.

It is better to make every day a special day and enjoy happiness and fruition while you can. To be a life enricher, you have to do it now. Make that choice and be a person who imparts something positive.

SELF STARTER

List two wrong choices you made but that paid off
in unexpected ways. How did you benefit in the
end?

In trying to make the right choices, your own soft bed may
sometimes be your most serious impediment in seeking success. You have to get out of it first, when it's much more
tempting to turn over and snooze a while longer. Your choices
of goals are not the end all and be all. They are simply steps
to success. Every goal reached has to be replaced by a new
one, otherwise your motivation will cease. If you set the goal
too far out and that's your only one, you will become discouraged before you reach it. In a sense, it is possible to
choose the right goals, but fail to choose intermediate goals
along the way. The best formula is one that incorporates intermediate goals that are realistic.

Rich and Jay found that many of the goals they initially
thought were unreachable were actually quite possible. The
answer, they decided, is that you have to believe you can attain
something you might not have considered earlier, if only to
test your capabilities.

People who are trying to decide whether or not to embark
on a certain venture in life are often discouraged because the
plans do not seem all that promising. "I just couldn't see all
that much fire in the idea" is a typical excuse for choosing
not to take the leap. However, many people find that future
achievement often lies, not in a flaming beginning, but in fan-
ning a small spark that can grow and grow and in the end
ignite the fire of success.

It is fashionable today to have "systems" of business accomplishment, especially in the corporate world. These are
expressed in books, in seminars, and in other media. People
rush to learn about a system and then pretty soon are dashing
off in a different direction to learn a newer system that has
come into vogue. Be wary about succumbing to the fashionable systems approach to life, realizing that success has many
different interpretations, depending upon the individual, the
location, the social structure, and dozens of other factors.

The importance of having a positive attitude cannot be over-emphasized. It can be summarized in one sentence: The winner sees an answer in every problem; the loser sees a problem in every answer.

Promises, Promises

It is an interesting—certainly noteworthy—trend when we see giant corporations wrestling today with choices that are in effect much like those of an individual trying to select various goals on the road to success. Like a young man courting the girl of his dreams, American companies are making you promises that they hope they can keep. Wooing your favor, as well as your pocketbook, are banks, airlines, insurance companies, auto makers, hotel chains, computer marketers, and appliance manufacturers, to name just a few. The phrases they tout are "extended warranty," "money-back guarantee," "quality assurance," and "customer satisfaction."

Why is it commercially fashionable these days to jump on the customer-indemnity bandwagon? One reason is that sales competition has stiffened in the marketplace. Another is the realization that the additional cost of the warranty or the guarantee offered is more than outweighed by the additional sales reaped through these proclamations of responsibility.

Individuals can benefit, too, by declaring personal fidelity and a guarantee of integrity when applying for jobs, seeking positions of responsibility in their communities, or running for public office. When they choose to take this path of honor on the way to hoped-for achievement, however, they had better also choose to be honest with themselves and determine just how far they can really assert their virtues.

Another corporate trend that affects individual job performance is what we refer to as the *service surge*. Some very curious activities are being reported these days in the marketplace, among them: Tellers in a bank in Pennsylvania are smearing their glasses with Vaseline before filling out deposit slips; a supermarket in Connecticut gives refunds to customers on unsatisfactory products purchased at *other* markets; salespeople at an electronics store in Massachusetts wear gloves while using keyboards to demonstrate floor models to prospective buyers of computers.

Why?

These organizations, like many others soliciting increased consumer business, are placing new emphasis on customer service by training employees to learn how to listen, ask questions, identify customer problems, and resolve complaints. Hence, the bank tellers can relate better to older patrons with failing eyesight, the supermarket can back up its publicized motto that "the customer is always right," and the the computer salespeople can better relate to the needs of prospective buyers who may be "all thumbs" when it comes to operating unfamiliar machines.

The companies mentioned—and many, many more—are taking these steps voluntarily, but when you look behind the scenes, you will find that they have done their homework before making their decision. According to a national business publication, nine out of ten dissatisfied customers will never buy again from an offending company, 65 percent of the average retailer's business comes from present customers, and securing a new customer costs five times as much as keeping an old one.

The lesson here is that making a choice can be a very difficult and complex function. If you don't do your homework and evaluate the situation necessitating the choice, you may never really understand what action to take.

The Consumer's Bill of Rights

The changes taking place in the marketplace and the nature of goals established by private companies that serve the public led Jay Van Andel and Rich DeVos some years ago to describe what they refer to as "The Consumer's Bill of Rights." It is essential for individuals to keep these points in mind as they try to shape their careers and reflect on what may be demanded of them on the job, whether as employees or as entrepreneurs.

Among the rights consumers must have are the right
* to be a free consumer

- to benefit from competition
- to choose from many markets
- to personal service
- to make their own buying decisions and selections
- to decide where, when, and how to buy
- to patronize those who serve them best

The consumer must have the right to cast consumer ballots through the purchase of goods and services from individuals and companies who satisfy consumer wants in the manner consumers alone determine best.

The Impact of Timing

For the individual as well as for the company, timing is a crucial factor. It is vital in establishing a lifestyle, selecting a career, raising a family, and all other aspects of life. When do you plan something? When do you start? How do you determine what is the right or wrong time for each phase of what you are doing, or intend to be doing?

You can't worry yourself to death over the timing, since very often that is out of your control. Looking back in hindsight, it is always easy to say, ''Oh, I should have started earlier,'' or ''It would have been better if we had waited until circumstances improved.'' Sometimes things just happen and you never really know whether the timing was good, bad, or in between. The important thing is to have an outlook that keeps you in action and lets you get back in proper balance if the timing is off and you tip too far one way or the other.

The most crtical aspect of timing is not whether the external circumstances are exactly right, but whether *you* are ready. Are you prepared to take the time, make the necessary sacrifices, expend enough energy, and undertake sufficient work to achieve your goal? There is no easy, simple method for tapping into success. ''Take the business we are in for example,'' says Rich DeVos. ''We offer a well conceived and an affordable opportunity. You might even call it a 'package,' because all of the ingredients are there for the start of a successful program. Yet that is no guarantee that people who take this opportunity are really ready for it on the day that it comes to them. We have found that some people stumble for months, even years, before they finally get moving in the right direction and become successful. And thus it is with all other opportunities in life, even the ones that are the best formulated.''

Timing can be very deceptive, very tricky. If you are in a business in Maine that sells snow shovels, you would be considered overoptimistic, to say the least, if you tried to peddle them in July. But wait a minute! Some enterprising entrepreneurs have started Christmas shops in *summertime* vacation regions and racked up unbelievable sales. They have done so on the theory that a rather contradictory type of timing can work for them: Many tourists spend their time shopping when on summer vacations, they look for bargains, and they cannot escape the nostalgia of Christmas, even when the thermometer is in the eighties. So who says you can't sell snow shovels in the summer?

SELF STARTER

Think about it, and list two other kinds of products or services that have been successfully marketed out of season.

Delegation

Hand in hand with timing is the matter of delegation. The more you climb the ladder of success, the more you have to schedule your time so that you put your capabilities to the best use. Take bookkeeping as an example. Keeping financial and statistical records is obviously of prime importance in business operations, regardless of their size. But bookkeeping is also essential in personal endeavors. If you just hate struggling with the books, you do have alternatives. You can choose to hire an outside professional, as in the case of tax returns. You can browbeat a qualified member of your family into doing the job, as in the matter of getting help from a spouse or child who has professional experience in bookkeeping. Or you can take the bull by the horns and attend a continuing education course at the local high school and learn how to do the job properly all by yourself.

In any case, the basic question you have to ask yourself is this: Can I attain my goals more effectively if I turn the assignment over to someone else? Usually it is better to delegate certain jobs—the kind you consider to be chores—if you can thus free yourself to undertake more fruitful and rewarding tasks. What do you do when you are starting off in a business and don't have the personnel under you or the funds to delegate purely functional tasks? Then choices are even more vital because you have to decide which chores to leave undone or at least minimize. Isn't it a better choice to live with sloppy bookkeeping and have good customer relations than to maintain perfect books but have no customers?

We all have to prioritize our activities because we just don't have enough time to cover all the bases. There's a limit to how much energy we can expend and how much sleep we can do without. If we're lucky enough to join forces with someone else and be mutually respecting partners, at least we can rotate some of the work out front and some of it behind the scenes. Partners can complement each other and ideally they do so. Partnerships are like marriages. If you can see eye to eye and agree and each carry your share of the burden, they work. But if that doesn't happen, then you are better off choosing to stay single and independent.

When you are alone in an enterprise—whether personal or career-oriented—and have no business partner or counselor to help you in making hard choices and tough decisions, we urge you to bear in mind that you can always have a partnership with God. "Doubt is the disease of this inquisitive, restless age," said Billy Graham. "It is the price we pay for our advanced civilization. But as the most beautiful light is born of darkness, so the faith that springs from conflicting choices is often the strongest and the best. . . .When God granted man the power of choice, he took the risk of man choosing evil instead of good; death instead of life; and self-destruction instead of salvation."

Søren Kierkegaard, a noted nineteenth-century Danish philosopher, composed a prayer to strengthen his resolve whenever he had to make a difficult decision: "Lord, I have to make a serious choice and I'm afraid I'll make the wrong one. But I cannot put it off. So I shall make it and trust you to forgive me if the choice is wrong. And, Lord, I'll trust you, too, to help make things right afterward.''

CHAPTER
8

Magic Selections

"To be able to choose the line of greatest advantage instead of yielding in the path of least resistance is the essence of freedom."

—George Bernard Shaw

In the 1970s, Dr. Jean Meyer, president of Tufts University in Medford, Massachusetts, was greatly concerned about the apparent inability of young people to come to grips with basic choices in life. "The ability to arrive at complex decisions," wrote Meyer, "should be the hallmark of the educated person. In this tense, ever more crowded, ever more interdependent world, decision-making is becoming more and more crucial . . . the future of the human race will depend upon whether our graduates, citizens of the greatest democracy on earth, members of the most highly developed technological society in the world, have the wisdom and the courage to make, and to carry out, the right decisions."

At about the same time, another educator, Professor Gordon Porter Miller, of Columbia University, was facing the same situation after spending eight years developing a highly successful training course for people of all ages in all walks of life. Speaking as director of the Decision-Making Program of the College Entrance Examination Board, he said, "Life is full of choices, and regardless of age, background, or personal circumstances, people find it difficult to make decisions. The sad fact of the matter is that little has been done in schools, colleges, families, and business settings to equip us to make choices wisely. We may go to college, get married, raise a family, follow a career, relocate, and retire—all critical or life-shaping decision opportunities—without ever actually making a well considered, well informed choice."

The tragic results of poor decision-making came to him, not through theoretical studies but after lengthy, hard-core experience while serving as an active guidance counselor. He studied the way young people were using information to make choices regarding education, careers, and lifestyles, and reached the conclusion that, ''regardless of the quality of their information, they tended to go along with societal expectations or with what had been done before by others like them. Rarely did they make decisions based on what was important to them. And frequently they actually let others make decisions for them. . . .What these individuals lacked was a *process for deciding,* some way of integrating available information with their personal needs and priorities.''

The Techniques of Choosing

Psychologists are familiar with a word, *abulia,* which comes from the Greek and means literally ''without will.'' It is used in sociological evaluations to refer to a strong inability or unwillingness on the part of an individual to make decisions. Some psychologists think that the problem of abulia, as an actual disorder, is widespread, triggered at least in part by the unconscious understanding that choices beget risks.

The ancients were said to have practiced a curious procedure for making vital choices, particularly in the world of political and governmental matters. They discussed their options while drunk; reconsidered their decision the next day, when sober; then reversed the process; and finally agreed with the choice that seemed most logical after these thinking and drinking bouts.

To be able to make choices decisively, if not always wisely, is said by sociologists and historians to be a sensible indication of personal growth. We do not grow by default, nor do we grow by playing it safe and hoping that all will turn out well. We grow (or fail to grow) because of the decisions we make, whether because of internal beliefs or external pressures and realities. Only thus do we reach new plateaus in our lives and our work. When we make our own choices, rather than allowing relatives, friends, or associates to make decisions for us, we are strengthening a powerful tool that will further our own future development. When we fail to make decisions—often a much poorer strategy than making decisions that are wrong—we actually weaken our capabilities.

The Power to Overcome

"Real growth comes from within," wrote two psychologists in a book, *How to Be Your Own Best Friend.* "Unfortunately, we create working hypotheses when we are young and then we don't revise them as we mature and gain experience. We try to fit new experiences into old, outmoded slots."

As the book explains, there are plenty of people having a wonderful time with their lives, but they don't talk about it because they are busy doing it. The source of happiness and achievement is within us, not outside. Most people haven't begun to tap their own potential and are operating way below capacity. You have to make a fundamental choice: Do you want to lift yourself up or put yourself down? Many people are literally their own worst enemy.

A study showed that children who are classified as low achievers in school tend to remain low achievers. But if you treat young people as what they *could* be rather than what they are, then there is a good chance that they will improve. The same is true of adults and what they decide they are—or are not. Far too many come up with all kinds of excuses why they cannot make meaningful decisions that will result in specific self-improvement.

Physical disabilities have been cited as one of the most widespread types of excuses. How valid are they? Consider the following list of myths and facts:

Myth: The lives of people with disabilities are totally different from those of other people.

Fact: People with disabilities carry on many normal activities. They go to school, get married, work in careers, have families, laugh, cry, get angry, plan, and dream just like everyone else.

Myth: All people who use wheelchairs are chronically ill.

Fact: A person may choose to use a wheelchair for a variety of reasons, none of which may have anything to do with illness.

Myth: People with disabilities are much more comfortable being with their own kind.

Fact: Years of grouping disabled persons in separate schools and institutions have reinforced this total misconception. Today, more and more people with disabilities have chosen to live and work in the mainstream.

These are just a few of the illusions that persist, and with which the disabled must cope in addition to their physical or psychological problems. However, it is important that persons with disabilities not only cope with, but *overcome* the barriers erected by society. When you see, work with, or hear about people with disabilities, you are automatically faced with a choice, whether you have anticipated it or not: You can either accept the myth, or you can understand the fact.

Having known so many people with disabilities who have more than earned their right to a normal life, we deeply hope you will choose the fact.

A Sense of Values

Three years after being implicated in the disastrous Watergate scandal that forced the resignation of President Nixon, John Ehrlichman wrote about his attempts to grapple with his own derelictions. "I now realize," he wrote in an article in *New York* magazine in May 1976, "that I lived 50 years of my life without ever really coming to grips with the very basic question of what is and is not important to me. . . .I've begun a process that my own kids began almost from the beginning: developing a personal sense of values. I'm a beginner!"

It is sad, but true, that too many people are beginners when it comes to making decisions about their sense of values. Studies at the College of Education of Ohio University listed three supportive ways in which values had to be decided upon in order to make them applicable and forceful:

1. *A Value Must Be Chosen Freely.* The decisions of an individual cannot reflect his or her own true values if some

force has been exerted to arrive at conclusions. Therefore, a true value is one chosen without physical or psychological coercion, including group or peer pressure.

2. *A Value Must Be Chosen from Alternatives.* For a value to be chosen freely, one must be aware of the optional values that are possible and practical.

3. *A Value Must Be Chosen After Considering the Consequences.* Individuals must be well aware of the price they will have to pay for holding a certain value. Both the risks and the benefits have to be recognized. Henry David Thoreau, for example, chose certain very precise values in life and in one instance was aware that he would be jailed for failing to pay taxes that he believed were supporting an unjust war. He could be said to have possessed a true value since he was aware of the hazard when making his choice.

Do you know of other very hard choices in today's world that relate to the price required to uphold one's sense of values? Of course you do. Just think of the super-difficult choices faced by doctors and the families of terminally ill patients who decide that their loved ones should be taken off technological life-support systems; or how to handle elderly invalids who are in limbo: too sick to be in nursing homes, yet not sufficiently ill to be in hospital intensive-care units; or the decision not to try to sustain the lives of premature infants who are brain damaged and have no hope of survival.

Lewis B. Smedes, a theologian who served on the ethics committee of a large hospital in Southern California, wrote, "These are crises that keep serious doctors awake at night wondering whether they are making the right choices. But very often no one has a clear and simple answer. Is it right to stop expensive treatment on an elderly patient when the machine seems to be keeping a body alive after the person who once lived in it has gone? Is it right not to operate on a newborn baby when all the indications are that the baby will exist as a virtual vegetable even if the operation is successful?"

In such circumstances, one must turn to prayer. A particularly apt one is the "Serenity Prayer" adopted by Alcoholics

Anonymous for people wrestling with problems of alcohol and drug abuse:

> God grant me the serenity to accept the things I cannot change,
> The courage to change the things I can,
> And the wisdom to know the difference.

As Smedes also commented, "Now and then we all get into situations that seem to tell us that we are 'damned if we do and damned if we don't.' Other occasions seem to tell us that there simply is no right or wrong thing to do about them, but only a somewhat better thing, or a less bad thing. These are times when we feel as if we are thrown on our own, and we may end up wondering whether *anyone* can know for sure that he or she has made a right choice."

American theologian and philosopher Reinhold Niebuhr wrote that people faced with making critical choices have three responsibilities:

1. To initiate prompt and positive action.
2. To make an honest response to the situation in which they find themselves
3. To account for their actions and their decisions

He said that the choices made by responsible people are really their own, not a consensus of what their peers might make; that the decisions reflect what is happening to them, or around them; and that they have logical reasons for their considered choices, not merely whims or excuses that things have always been done this way before. Many times, making a responsible choice can transform an undesirable situation into a good one, even though the person making the choice may have to accept some sacrifices. But one thing is certain: We should do our best to avoid choosing *not* to choose.

SELF STARTER

List two recent occasions in which you decided to let things ride and *not* make any choice at all. Looking back on it, do you regret that negative decision? Why?

The Power to Change

A philosopher commented that "life too often presents us with a choice of evils, rather than of good," an outlook that has been expressed many times over by writers and speakers. One of these exponents of evil was certainly the infamous Nazi, Joseph Goebbels, who had been a brilliant student at college and a man with every opportunity to choose good over evil. By the time he realized he had made a poor choice—if he ever did—it was too late to change.

Fortunately, most of us can make bad choices and later effect a dramatic change. Once you know what has caused some turbulent times in your life, you can learn to cope with the situation and flow with the changes, not fight them. We cannot say that changes don't apply to us. We must look at ourselves as others see us and do what needs to be done to adjust. We all know examples of defunct companies—even whole civilizations—that failed to adjust to change.

Even the most tragic, the most catastrophic situations can be changed if only dedicated individuals are willing to make very difficult choices that require supreme sacrifices. You may recall the story of the fierce tribe of Auca Indians some years ago. Five missionaries who tried to convert them were killed, but a later group of missionaries presevered and did manage to establish Christianity in this hostile land. Written in the diary of one of the missionaries who had been killed was this question about his ultimate goal: "If not I, *who* and if not now, *when?*"

Our power to change or to bring about changes in others often requires that we make some choices that are very difficult, very uncertain, or very unflattering to our ego. Here are six phrases that are meaningful:

- I was wrong.
- I am sorry.
- I need you.
- Thank you for what you did.
- I am proud of you.
- I love you.

If you are in the midst of trying to make changes and redress wrongs, be big enough to say forthrightly and without evasion just how you feel. Individuals are accountable for their choices and actions, and must be willing to take responsibility and accept rewards or punishments that follow as a natural consequence of their behavior. As has been said a number of times in similar ways, "Accountability is the glue that holds society together."

There is an unfortunate trend, which finds increasing numbers of people claiming that individuals should not be held accountable for their actions. The child who fails in school, for example, is poorly motivated. The habitual criminal is the fault of society. The public servants who cheat do so because they work in an immoral atmosphere where such actions are condoned. The employees who steal from their companies do so because they are grossly underpaid.

A famous psychologist even authored a best-seller proclaiming that man is not accountable for his behavior—it is the fault of the social and moral environment. But if no one is accountable, society itself will fail. No one will do any work or try to be honest if all people are judged to be equally good or bad, regardless of what they do or don't do.

The more that people have, the greater will be their accountability. Individuals are answerable at the different levels of life in which they find themselves. People with modest incomes are still responsible for the way they use money, even though the amounts may seem insignificant. People with only a few close friends are still accountable for their relationships to those few. Helen Keller could have insisted that life had dealt her a bad blow by making her both blind and deaf. But she had too high a respect for herself and held herself accountable for whatever she was able to do with her life, thus proving that it could be not only useful to society but inspiring to others.

In our roster of fine leaders and achievers in life who recognize the significance of accountability, few can surpass the late Arthur Ashe who said, ''I have always tried to be true to myself, to pick those battles I felt were important. My ultimate responsibility is to myself. I could never be anything else.''

Ashe was not only dynamic on the tennis court, but never hesitated to speak out for what he thought was right, even when he knew that his opinions would cause a backlash of rebuttals from members of his own race and from people in the world of sports where he had to function. He rubbed a great many people the wrong way, for instance, when he said, ''We need to address the deep-seated cynicism of coddled black public school athletes, many of whom are carried through school with inflated grades and peer group status that borders on deification. High school coaches need to be held accountable for the academic preparation of their would-be Michael Jordans.''

If people are held accountable, they must also be free to make their own choices. Accountability and freedom go hand in hand. When you can't be sure about a choice, you can at least be responsible.

The Litmus Test of Choices: Results

Dr. Smedes wrote that some people were convinced that the only way we can tell whether we have made a right choice is by evaluating the consequences. ''The test of right choices,'' he said, ''is results. It's as simple as that . . . if what we choose to do brings good results, we can be pretty sure that we are doing the right thing. Or, if what we are thinking about doing is likely to produce good results, we can be reasonably sure we will be choosing the right thing to do.''

Can you ever be sure? Not always. But one practical way to test whether you are heading in the right direction is to ask yourself these questions:

- Do I actually understand what might be good for me, in terms of results?

- Do my associates or family members or whoever may be involved in my choices know what is best for us all, collectively?

SELF STARTER

Can you name one choice that involved a moral or ethical decision within the past month? Within the past year?

Rights and Responsibilities

"Some time ago," says Jay Van Andel,

we published a short text that made manifest our belief in all people created by God, regardless of faith, heritage, race, color, sex, age, or any other characteristics. It stated the following six rights:

1. The right of each individual to achieve personal stature
2. The right of each individual to choose to pursue his or her own goals
3. The right of individuals to have a unique interest in life and pursue those causes they hold dear
4. The right to private ownership, whether of property, material goods, or ideas
5. The right to choose, voluntarily, to participate or not, as desired, in any aspect of life
6. The right to receive rewards based on performance, thus breaking the bonds of slavery and poverty in whatever form

We emphasized the fact that with every right there came a responsibility—that you have the right to choose your own goals, but you also have the responsibility to help others to achieve goals and to uplift other human beings as much as possible.

To these rights, we would also add the right to privacy.

Too often, though, in this technological age when electronic snooping is so widespread, privacy lies beyond an individual's capacity for choice. A decade or so ago, an article in the *New York Times* announced that the Internal Revenue Service was about to "test whether computerized information about the lifestyles of American families can be used to identify individuals who fail to pay their income taxes." The data included descriptions of neighborhoods, how long families had lived in them, and the models and years of the cars they owned, among other facts.

As related in the *Times,* the information was to be compiled and supplied by private marketing companies that gather information from public sources such as telephone companies, motor vehicle agencies, and the Census Bureau. It all sounded like an excerpt from George Orwell's classic book, *1984,* which depicted massive invasions of privacy. Since that time, technology has expanded so rapidly that invasion of our privacy has become one of the top problems Americans have to face today.

How to Sell Yourself and Your Viewpoints

Rich DeVos points out that there are three kinds of people in the world:

1. The Number Ones, the achievers who are the doers and shakers, the leaders.
2. The Number Twos, who are always looking for someone to follow and on whom they hope they can unload stories about what they might have been, "if only. . . "
3. The Number Threes, who have at best gone off somewhere to "do their thing" or at worst have simply copped out of life.

It is likely that you hope to be in the Number One category—if not right now, then fairly soon. But you have to do a selling job. First, you have to sell yourself on you. Once convinced that you have shaped up as expected, you then have to sell others. The choices you make will determine, in part, how well you accomplish this feat. Choices become doubly important when you are on your way upward and have to make decisions that will affect your life, lifestyle, and ultimate goals. You can go a long way down the road in the wrong direction before realizing that you have to reshape your thinking and adjust your sights.

We suggest nine rules for selling yourself:

1. Protect your good name.
2. Tell the truth, even if it hurts.
3. Keep the right company.
4. Keep your promises.
5. Stick to your principles.
6. Beware of compromising.
7. Don't be afraid to say no.
8. Accentuate the positive.
9. Be persistent.

Although you could consider these guidelines to open the door to a better life, there is no real formula for success other than your own energy and the capabilities and personal power you have to draw on. But you have to think positively and do your homework and find the options.

One of the best pieces of advice we can give is to suggest that you consider yourself an *entrepreneur,* even though you may not be in your own business and never intended to be. An entrepreneur is like an artist. He can look at an everyday thing—a person, place, or situation—and see something that other people don't see. He will have innovative ideas about ordinary circumstances. This was the thrust of an article that appeared in *Nation's Business,* explaining that the entrepreneur, like the artist, has the ability to transform and enhance his environment by applying creativity and imagination. While the artist uses a brush and palette, the entrepreneur wields a pencil and paper or perhaps a personal computer.

True entrepreneurs look at the world with what might be referred to as *creative dissatisfaction.* Put another way, they feel that there isn't a thing in the world that cannot be improved. Everyone has the freedom to make choices that can bring about improvements—in income, lifestyles, jobs, family life, recreational pursuits, and just about every facet of life. The point is that you are surrounded by opportunities to make choices that will shake loose the mental cobwebs, trigger a real brainstorm, and put you on a higher plateau in life.

Is now the time to activate yourself?

Heed the words of one of America's most famous poets and philosophers, Ralph Waldo Emerson, "This time, like all times, is a very good one—if we but know what to do with it."

CHAPTER
9

And in Conclusion . . .

"Leaders are called upon again and again to make weighty choices, some that affect the very core of a nation. I found that it was easier to make such choices at the end of the day, when I could sleep on them, rather than having to act immediately."
—Sir Winston Churchill

This is not an ending, it is a beginning.

Believe in that old saying, tired and trite though it may seem to some: This is the first day of the rest of your life. There are no endings as long as choices still have to be made. What is the first thing we have to do when we wake up each day? We must choose whether to get up or stay in bed for awhile. Perhaps the choice is all but preordained for most people. They simply must get up and get ready to go to work. Yet, even so, a few people have abruptly made adversarial decisions in this fleeting instant. They have decided that, no they are not going to get up and go to work. This is the day they are going to quit the job they do not like and later get another one. Or become an entrepreneur and launch their own enterprise. Or run away from an oppressive lifestyle and take a long overdue vacation.

It comes as no surprise that some people make instant career decisions that may seem quite out of character. Surveys tell us that one of the most common reasons why people are dissatisfied with life is because they hate their jobs. They find the workplace dull, or the pay is meager, or management offers little hope of advancement. The sudden realization that one is boxed in, as though trapped in a room without a door, can sometimes be a blessing in disguise. It motivates the person to consider options and come to grips with critical decisions that otherwise would never have been made.

People are basically afraid to make certain kinds of decisions until they are either activated by a greater fear or emboldened by a newfound faith. Dr. Norman Vincent Peale urged people to develop a positive attitude toward themselves and others, which can be achieved by broadening one's personal outlook, exercising enthusiasm, learning to listen, and using one's intellect.

What do you really want out of life?

Henry David Thoreau put it this way: "Many men go fishing all their lives without ever knowing it is not the fish they are after."

A Checklist of Choices

Jay Van Andel and Rich DeVos have always been great believers in making lists of their goals and deadlines. These are road maps in the journey along their chosen career paths. As in the case of all maps, the routes are subject to revisions as better paths are envisioned or the conditions of the existing routes change. Thus, they are continually being reviewed and updated. However, they are careful to maintain overall guidelines that may be modified and perfected, but that remain more or less constant. The list that follows, somewhat edited and condensed, will be of help to readers who have followed these pages patiently for nine chapters and still are willing to consider what Rich and Jay have to say about life and work and relationships. We suggest that you use the list as a catalyst for compiling your own personal map, modifying, adding, or deleting entries to suit your own goals and expectations.

The components are not necessarily in order of sequence or importance, but should be rearranged to reflect your own priorities and needs.

- Write the choices and options available for any particular venture or situation. Be as specific as possible.
- Frame your objectives in a positive way, rather than as a negative problem. "Partly sunny" is always better than "partly cloudy."
- Include at least a few goals (or subgoals) that are enjoyable to attain and that can spark your enthusiasm.
- Make sure you really know what the choices are. If not, review your goals and destinations.

- Strive to be centered, bringing goals into sharp focus rather than being scattered and hazy.
- Do your homework. Some of the worst errors in decision-making come from overlooking pieces of the puzzle.
- Identify all of your resources that can be applied to the goals at hand.
- List alternatives and possible modifications. Some options may not be immediately apparent or may need clarification.
- When considering options, be realistic about past failures and successes and your capabilities.
- Heed your instincts and gut reactions, but also know the difference between intuition and wishful thinking.
- Take small action steps first, rather than a quantum leap, and implement your decisions in increments.
- Discuss the choices and alternatives with others who are, or might be, concerned with the decision, and later the outcome of it, but at the same time make up your own mind.
- Try to be objective in appraising the situation, possibly conferring with someone qualified to give an opinion.
- Anticipate what will happen in the case of each possible choice or decision.
- Don't rush into a choice, but don't sit back too long before taking action. Set a realistic time limit and deadlines.
- Don't get hung up on the results, after you have made a decision and are having second thoughts about it.
- Consider your choice in light of who and what you are, not on what someone else might think or do.
- Bear in mind that, in most cases, decisive action is better than no action at all.
- Don't confuse your decision with an outcome or result that occurs only after you have made a choice.

APPENDIX

Supportive Material for the Chapters on Choices

"When we have considered and made decisions in regard to each and every one of the choices at hand, we are always astonished to learn that there are still more choices just down the road and out of sight."
—Woodrow Wilson

Acknowledgments

The author is indebted, first and foremost, to Jay Van Andel and Rich DeVos for the time and thought they devoted on so many occasions to interviews and compilations of their speeches and writings over the years. He also gives special thanks to Jay's daughter, Nan, for scheduling the many meetings and discussions and for her patience in reading the manuscript and making suggestions, to Ken McDonald for coordinating the information-gathering sessions, and to Ted Benjamin, who designed and produced the lavishly illustrated history, *Commitment to Excellence*.

Choice Calculator

This tool will help you decide which choice is likely to be the best when making important decisions. The calculations help the user to line up the most probable options and then "computerize" the decision. Examples of the kinds of options listed on the *calculator:*

What I *need . . . don't need*

What I *want . . . don't want*

What I *like . . . don't like*

What I can *afford . . . cannot afford*

What I would be *comfortable* with . . . *uncomfortable* with

What others *prefer . . . don't prefer . . .* to have me choose

What in the short run is *best . . . worst*

What in the long run is *best . . . worst*

What rewards are *most obvious . . . least obvious*

Previous *similar* choices that *worked . . . did not work*

Time Factor
- Deadline

- Best time to make choice
- Worst time to make choice

Personal Factor
- Others affected by choice
- Others who might help make choice

Location Factor
- Best place to make choice
- Worst place to make choice

Communications Factor
- Private decision
- Public decision
- Written or verbal

Choices: The Magic Square to Personal Success

```
C H O I C E S
H           U
O           C
I    YOU    C
C           E
E           S
S U C C E S S
```

Most people who think they would like to achieve a measure of success—whether in a career, business, personal life, or in any other way—are usually content with trying to accomplish just a little bit more to be satisfied. Some, with more drive and ambition, set their goals at doubling their objectives, ranging from increases in income to the making of friends or the improvement of their stature in the community.

Believing that any such attempts require additional expenditures of time, work, and energy, most of these would-be achievers set their sights too low. What they do not realize is that they can hope for goals beyond their fondest dreams by using a formula that is almost effortless once it is understood and applied.

We call it the *Magic Square,* based on a simple, realistic

method of knowing how to make the right choices at the right time in order to achieve the desired success.

Anyone who has studied mathematics knows that to *square* a number is to multiply it by itself. Thus, while four plus four is only eight, four *squared* is sixteen. The procedure involves simple arithmetic—no more difficult than adding or multiplying.

Think of this formula as you make choices and set your sights on success. Your first choice on the road to achievement is to repeat over and over to yourself that you are going to *multiply* your goals, not simply add a few minor elements by way of improvement.

The Seven Pillars of Choices

Whenever you make a choice, you bring into action seven vital elements that can work in your favor:

C *Concerns* that are important and have necessitated choices in the first place

H *Hopes* that inspire you to aim higher and upgrade your stature in life

O *Opportunities* that have been revealed and can be seized if you make the right choices

I *Independence* to strive for a goal on your own and reach the place where you want to be

C *Capabilities* that have lain fallow and can be energized by positive decisions

E *Ethics* whose nature and extent keep you on course when you might otherwise stray

S *Sources* of new strength that are available when you decide which route to follow

How Good Are You at Making Choices That Lead to Success?

The following true-or-false test focuses on some of the areas of choice and decision that are important and that have been discussed in this book. Carefully consider the following statements as criteria for making money in your career or profession. Circle *T* if the statement is true, and *F* if it's false. Then find out whether you agree with Jay Van Andel and Rich DeVos, who have become millionaires many times over by making the right choices.

1. Choose several ventures to work at once.   [T] [F]

2. Emulate lifestyles of millionaires.   [T] [F]

3. A college degree is needed to become rich.   [T] [F]

4. Delegate the running of business to others.   [T] [F]

5. You can make money with money.   [T] [F]

6. Work hard for short periods and then take it
    easy for long periods.   [T] [F]

7. Take every shortcut to the top you can.   [T] [F]

8. Channel every waking thought to success.   [T] [F]

Now check your answers against the reasoning of the au-
thors of this little quiz as they evaluate each statement.

1. Choose several ventures to work at once. F.

This is what we call the *tycoon syndrome*. Sure, it works
sometimes for certain types of entrepreneurs, but the situation
is like that of an entertainer on the stage who attempts to
juggle many different items at once. It all looks great, until he
makes one slip and the whole act falls apart. To be successful
in the long run, you have to focus on one venture, one goal
at a time. Then channel all of your efforts in that direction.
President Harry Truman was right on target when he stated
that *single-mindedness* was one of the greatest factors in attaining success. Or, as someone else phrased it, "When you
have a winning horse, ride it."

2. Emulate lifestyles of millionaires. F.

Never try to emulate the wealthy before you have the money
to do so. People who say they have to put on a good front
and *appear* to be wealthy in order to become wealthy are
likely to end up with nothing but huge bills. People succeed
when they present themselves as they really are and are honest
about their status and their goals. It is all too common to hear
an employee say, "Pay me more and I'll work harder." That
request is all backward. The true statement should be "Work
harder and we'll pay you more."

There is one aspect of the above idea, however, that should
be kept in mind: You can often become successful by learning
and emulating the *work habits* of people who are successful.

3. A college degree is needed to become rich. F.

You do not need a college degree, or even a partial college
education, to be successful. That does not mean that you
should avoid study and learning. Five years from now, you

will be the same person you are today, except for the people you associate with and the books you read. Some 4,000 years ago the wise King Solomon proclaimed, "Any enterprise is built by wise planning; it becomes strong through common sense; and it profits wonderfully by keeping abreast of the facts." He also said, "A dull axe requires great strength. Be wise and sharpen the blade."

There is no doubt that we learn by reading about ways in which others have become successful and can then profit from their ideas and methods and concepts. Know-how is a guide to the top. Expand your know-how by reading, listening to tapes, and absorbing knowledge.

4. Delegate the running of business to others. F.

Although we have often advised, "Delegate or stagnate," we do not advocate delegating the *running* of your business to others, but only those activities that are nonproductive. You cannot delegate the creative, managerial responsibilities that determine how successful you are, or will be.

5. You can make money with money. F.

In one way, of course, you can make money with money through smart investing. In the long run, however, you can only make money by investing a great deal of time and energy, as well as dollars. So take Mr. Truman's advice. Be single-minded and concentrate all of your efforts in the area where you can make most of your money. If you try to make money with money but do not devote enough time to your primary venture, then you are likely to squander or certainly dilute, your investment.

6. Work hard for short periods and then take it easy for long periods. F.

This is what we call *the stop-and-go syndrome.* Many people practice this course of action. They work very hard, almost to the point of exhaustion, then take long periods to rest. Your best approach is to set a steady speed and stick with it. When you work every day at a planned pace, you become an expert and a winner. Sure, you should stop once in a while to evaluate yourself, take a breather, and look at what you are doing in an overview. But do not interrupt your work so long that you break the pace.

The Reverend Robert Schuller advised, "When you approach realizing a dream, start a new one because you must change the 'is' to the 'ought' or you'll slow down and maybe never get started again.'' Some people settle for too little too soon and then find it difficult to build their momentum again. Choose your goal and then keep at it steadily.

Success is a journey, not a destination.

7. Take every shortcut to the top you can.   F.

Many so-called shortcuts are either unethical or downright dishonest, as has been demonstrated only too tragically by some of the "bright" young men of Wall Street who decided they could earn huge incomes by shortcutting the established rules of the investment profession. There is no shortcut to success. Most such routes turn out to be dead ends. Businessmen often exchange ideas with each other about better ways of running a venture. But too often it turns out that they are all exchanging *unproven* ideas, are indulging in wishful thinking, and have not found shorter, quicker ways of attaining their objectives after all.

8. Channel every waking thought to success.   T.

There is absolutely no doubt that those who would achieve goals should focus their thoughts continuously and positively on eventual success. The Bible reminds us, "As a man thinks, so is he." What you accomplish depends upon the way your mind functions. "What the mind can conceive, man can achieve because the mind is all powerful." If you believe this, you will see it. When your mind focuses on a goal, you will achieve it. But if your mind is divided, your goal will be fractured. Again, it is a matter of being *single-minded*.

The choices are yours—and so are the outcomes.

The Winner's Checklist

If you want to be a winner, you have to *think* like a winner whenever you make difficult or critical choices. Here are some ways to condition yourself for success:

- Interpreting your intuition, the gut feelings that certain options can be right for you, or wrong
- Cultivating patience, a successful way to reduce risks by taking the time to evaluate situations and then anticipating what can happen when you select any of several options that may be open
- Discovering the value of homework through a simple formula for compiling facts effortlessly, learning quickly, and then applying knowledge to your advantage
- Understanding competition in such a way that it becomes a positive force in your life, not an obstacle
- Overcoming your fear of stress, which, instead of being a dangerous and disruptive force, can be controlled and made to work in your favor
- Discovering just who you are and what you are, and what your capabilities can be, in order to attain the greatest goals with the fewest restraints
- Familiarizing yourself with the "hand-of-cards" concept, which emphasizes that the *way* you play a hand of cards you are dealt is far more important than *what* cards you were dealt, and applying this to life situations

- Understanding the nature and scope of choices, the most prevalent activity in life, and learning how to recognize them, set priorities, and bet on the right ones at the right time
- Paying true respect to history and a thorough examination of pertinent peoples and cultures faced with earth-shaking choices from earliest times to the present
- Discovering how to turn the negatives completely around and transform adversity into advantage
- Preparing yourself always to pursue the positive, at the same time unlocking the secrets of inspiration, motivation, and productive action

Your Trip to Success

Dr. Robert Schuller, the noted theologian and creator of the philosophy of *possibility thinking* has compiled a beneficial exercise for readers who need to make personal choices about their lives and careers. Dr. Schuller's theory of possibility thinking is based on the idea that when you make major choices in life, you are willing to risk the possibility of failure for the possibility of success.

He envisions the power of an idea as being something that "wants to take a trip," or become activated. The planning of the trip takes place in ten parts.

Ten Points for Planning Your Trip to Success

1. *The Destination.* Where is the idea going to take me? Where does the road lead? To what destination will it bring me at the end of my life?
2. *The Journey.* Don't get loaded down with a lot of heavy-weight baggage—negative thoughts of discouragement, frustration, failure, and humiliation. Take a positive outlook about the journey ahead.
3. *The Companions.* What marks a great idea is the kind of support it attracts. What kind of people does it attract to accompany you—people who are positive?
4. *The Cost.* Not only the financial cost, but the cost of

pride if you try and fail. The better the journey, the higher the cost.

5. *The Passage.* The various passages: beginning, second or striving, third or arriving. Each has its own problems and rewards.

6. *The Adventure.* When you run into problems and set-backs and roadblocks, look upon them as part of a great adventure. Have courage, which is not the absence of fear, but looking into the unpredictable and still daring to move ahead.

7. *The Map.* The map is your philosophy of life, the pos-sibility thinker's creed. The motivation never to quit.

8. *The Crew.* No matter where you go, you won't go alone. If an idea is great, it should be born in prayer, and that means that God goes with you. He is your guide, your pilot, as well as your crew.

9. *The Ticket.* You buy the ticket and that pays the way. But no ticket ever took anybody anywhere on its own. The ticket is your decision, your choice to take the trip.

10. *The Passport.* The final thing you need is the passport, your freedom to travel, to choose the goals, to climb as high as you want to.

"Listen the next time when an idea that's positive—that's a dream—comes into your mind," says Schuller. "See that idea as a potential trip and give it wings. You'll be afraid probably. You might fail, but remember this—ultimately life is a contradiction. Part of you wants security, but another part of you wants excitement, and the two are a contradic-tion. . . .Possibility thinking is the process of making a com-mitment to a positive dream."

Bibliography

The following books are listed as supplemental reading for anyone interested in knowing more about Jay Van Andel, Richard DeVos, their philosophies of life, or other inspirational and motivational guidelines.

Conn, Charles Paul. *An Uncommon Freedom*. Grand Rapids, Mich.: Fleming H. Revell Company, 1982.

———— *The Possible Dream*. Grand Rapids, Mich.: Fleming H. Revell Company, 1977.

———— *The Winner's Circle*. New York: Berkley Publishing Corporation, 1979.

Counihan, Jim. *Another Step*. St. Paul, Minn.: Jim Counihan Ministries, 1984.

Cross, Wilbur, and Olson, Gordon. *Commitment to Excellence*. Elmsford, N.Y.: The Benjamin Company, 1986.

DeVos, Richard M. *Believe!* Old Tappan, N.J.: Fleming H. Revell Company, 1975.

Peale, Norman Vincent. *The Power of Positive Thinking*. Englewood Cliffs, N.J.: Prentice Hall, 1952.

SELF STARTERS

Following are suggestions for making use of the **SELF STARTER** exercises scattered throughout the book. The numbers refer to the chapter and page on which each **SELF STARTER** is printed. The purpose is to help you think through your options and come up with a response that is meaningful and positive.

1-4 Consider any ventures you have completed or positions you have reached that you consider fulfilling and use those to judge what your criterion is for success. Think also about your hopes and dreams for the future and how you would relate them to your achievement goals.

1-6 We all know people who say, "I would have accomplished thus and so if the circumstances hadn't been what they were," or who proclaim that fate or bad luck played a part in what happened (or didn't happen) to them. List two or three people who come to mind quickly who fit into this "unfortunate circumstances" category. Then ask yourself whether perhaps you are prone to this kind of negative thinking upon occasion. The idea here is to isolate, identify, and then try to avoid these situations and outlooks.

1-7 What kinds of choices have you made so far today? What ones did you make yesterday? What was the biggest choice you made during the past week? The past month? The past year? Which ones could you have avoided making at all, and with what kinds of consequences? List your five most important choices in order of their degree of difficulty and their meaning to you today.

1-8 After you have responded to the S/S question, put the question in reverse and ask yourself, "What seemingly small choices have *other* people made that involved me and that later affected both of our lives more than we ever could have expected?" (Example: I decided to go to a movie instead of staying home to watch a sports event on TV. While there, I ran into Joe S. who said, "I want you to meet my friend here, Pete Jones, who just happens to be looking for a business partner with your kind of experience." The result was the formation of a firm that has been quite prosperous.)

1-9 "Roadblocks" could be such things as overcoming a serious physical handicap, trying to pass a college course that you never should have taken, working for a boss who was far too demanding, facing the threat of having to move to a community that was less attractive because of financial difficulties, competing for a job or promotion against a strong contender, or becoming involved in complicated litigation.

1-11 A good example of this kind of turnabout is the case of Arthur Nance. All but forced to go to law school by his father, a noted judge, he deliberately failed in his second year so he could go into the ministry, where he was eminently successful.

1-12 Most people really give little thought to the influence that relatives play—or might play—in their lives. Yet when they think about the matter, they realize that life could be quite different if they could associate more with certain family members and less with others. If you cannot easily pinpoint the ones who fit these roles, simply make a list of key relatives and give them each a rating, from *1* on the low, or negative, side to *10* on the high, or positive, side. Then ask yourself what opportunities you have to spend more time with the uppers and less with the downers.

1-14 When selecting the family you would choose to avoid, make sure you are not mistaking bickering for debating. Some people love to take issue with each other and get into very controversial discussions as a way of educating each other or determining positive courses of action. Many times these people seem to be arguing when, in reality, they are playing an acceptable game of open discussion.

1-15 Be wary, though, about families who are so passive that their members never make waves or open their mouths for fear of offending each other. Ask yourself whether their actions are strong, constructive, and positive, not weak and evasive.

1-17 After you have compiled some clippings and listed a few of the most disturbing situations, list some positive actions you think could be taken in the communities or neighborhoods involved to help remedy the problems and prevent their constant repetition in the future. Pinpointing problems is easy, but finding realistic solutions is an entirely different ball game.

1-18 If you are already married, be frank about ways in which you could be more supportive and more understanding. How could your spouse also effect improvements in these matters? If you are not yet married, how do you envision the duties and responsibilities of each partner in a marriage that would lead to a better and more meaningful union?

1-20 Examples can revolve around such matters as differences of opinion about governmental issues, personality conflicts, political clashes, the problem of the haves versus the have-nots, racial confrontations, zoning, environmental planning, labor/management hostilities, or issues involving big business versus small business. Ask yourself:

1. What was the original situation and condition?
2. When did the turning point occur?
3. What person(s) effected a change for the better?

2-26 It is hoped here that you can picture people you know who fit the "winner" and "loser" categories. If you find this difficult to do, however, you can achieve the same results by substituting people you know about, or have read about, with whom you might conceivably have become associated in some kind of enterprise, whether in business, public life, or community service. A tougher question to answer is this: "How would *they* have fared when associating with *you?*"

2-27 What you are really searching for here is the answer to this question: "What would I have done differently in past months or years if I had known then what I know now about my career, my position in society, or my lifestyle?" Bear in mind, though, that in some cases making a mistake is not always that bad. As this book discusses, some people who got in with the wrong crowd or fell victim to bad habits in their youth were able to become all that much stronger in later years for having fought their way out of disastrous situations.

2-29 List some situations in which you have improved yourself by competing with people who were more accomplished or more dedicated or more competitive than you were.

2-30 How well do you know these people you have selected? Did you ever associate these qualities with them before? Do you possess any of the same qualities, good or bad?

2-32 Have you used either, or both, of these experiences to good advantage in improving yourself and the way you tackle difficult conditions?

2-34 Once you have made the list, place the entries in order of priority. Then make notations to show how much time you estimate would be needed to attain these goals.

2-36 Trying to be honest with yourself and objective in your evaluation, decide which of these four people is most like you in the matter of faith and belief. If you are on the negative side of the picture, what could you do to change your thinking for the better?

2-40 Having read this far in *Choices with Clout,* what other books would you like to read that take a positive approach to life? If you need some ideas, a number of suggestions are included in the Bibliography on page 181.

3-46 Ask yourself honestly whether, in deciding what your priorities were, you selected them on the basis of things you *had* to do, whether you liked it or not, things you thought would be enjoyable to do, or things that would help you to improve yourself. One productive way to establish workable priorities is to schedule things you simply must do first and then follow them up with a reward—something you want to do.

3-49 *Why* was each of these achievements meaningful? Write down the answers as clearly and specifically as you can. Then ask yourself one more question: Would you change either the way you went about making the achievements or your evaluation of what was accomplished?

3-54 How realistically could you have anticipated the results and actually applied better judgment and foresight?

3-63 Now that you have described three goals, place them in order of priority, with a comparable rating of one to ten so you can compare their proportionate significance. Are any of these goals likely to change and, if so, why?

4-69 Were these health priorities based on advice and counsel personally given to you by doctors or other health authorities? If not, take the time to read current articles about each of the subjects you have listed.

4-73 If you want to make improvements but are just plain stuck when it comes to figuring out how, try this procedure: List five improvements you would *like* to make. Cross out the ones that seem impossible or unrealistic to attempt. For each one you have crossed out, add another. Continue this sequence until you end up with five that are possible, realistic, and attainable within a reasonable period of time. Try to select improvements that do not require major disruptions in your life (which might make the "atmosphere" even worse), such as moving to another town, changing jobs, or making large expenditures.

4-76 A popular and generally effective device is to schedule something you don't really want to do, followed by some kind of pleasant activity as a "treat," but only after you have completed the unpleasant task. Another trick, when you cannot complete a project on any given day, is to stop work when you are partway through a phase that is easy to continue the next day.

4-81 Once you have made a selection, list them in order of preference—from most preferable to least—if you had to spend a number of days working with them on a community project. Try to imagine how each of them would rate *you* in terms of outer and inner attractiveness.

5-88 If you have not done anything to help your community and are not sure what you could do that would be rewarding, look under *Volunteer* in your phone book. You may find a listing for *Volunteer Center* or the like. If you cannot find any such organization, call the local Chamber of Commerce. You should easily be able to locate someone who can send you a list of public service activities for which volunteers are needed. If you belong to a church, that is a primary source of information about voluntarism.

5-91 Take a pad and pencil. Note the action required. List the things you have to do. Determine where you can get help, if needed. If you require materials, equipment, information, or anything else that will expedite the action and get results, jot down what you have to get and where. Set a realistic time schedule. Then just do it!

5-95   In listing advantages and disadvantages, avoid those that relate too strongly to income and other financial matters. It is difficult to make monetary comparisons that are at all meaningful from country to country because of the enormous variations in the intrinsic "value" of money around the globe.

5-98   Be wary of focusing on a need that might be a fad, that is likely to be limited to your own personal opinions, that is costly, or that is overly specialized. Try to put yourself in the position of the loan officer in a bank to whom you would apply for funding, and consider what his reaction might be to the kind of business you hope to establish.

5-102   The person you select could be someone who had to buck the elements, as it were, because of a severe physical handicap, a lack of money, opposition by bureaucrats, political animosity, or strong family objections.

6-111   Look deep inside yourself and ask whether the sacrifices might not be forceful and inspirational factors, rather than drawbacks. Sacrifices can be like calories. You don't want to give up the goodies, but the end result makes you glad you did.

6-114   Sometimes, when people feel that they are being unfairly manipulated or the subject of bias, the best course of action is to go straight to the source of the negative output and try to determine *why* there is strong opposition. The answers might just provide the information needed to counter the critics successfully. A professional football quarterback never succumbs to the opposition. He *expects* it. And he then uses his wits to determine how to outmaneuver his foes.

6-117   Some of the personal freedoms that people mention are privacy, freedom from fear, physical security, opportunities to get away from it all for a while, and the chance to speak their minds without being ridiculed or accused of bias.

7-131 One way of stimulating ideas in response to this exercise is to look in the classified employment sections of newspapers and magazines. It is remarkable how sometimes even the most drab and boring kinds of drudgery can be described in the most glowing terms. When you make your two selections, be sure that you actually know what the jobs entail and how well they are compensated.

7-134 When you made the two choices you cite, did you think they were good choices? When did you decide they were poor choices? And when and how did you realize that they were really beneficial after all?

7-138 If you cannot think of anything specific that relates to your experience, ask your friends or family members for some examples. And look at the advertisements for bargains being unloaded by merchants at the end of each season.

8-145 If you had to reach these decisions again—or major ones like them—would you be inclined to ask for advice and counsel from someone else? If so, would you be more likely to turn to close friends and relatives or to professional experts in the subject fields concerned?

8-149 If you had decided to make two choices rather than let these matters slide, how greatly would the outcomes have been different?

8-152 When you made these two choices, did you have any feeling that either or both of them involved ethical or moral decisions? If not, how and at what time did the idea strike you that such might be the case?

Choices for Successful Communicators

In no other area of human experience will you find so many needs for choices as in commonplace personal communication. Daily—even hourly—you have to make choices about what you say or write or communicate by other means, or whether you will indeed communicate at all. The need is continuous, the range enormous. Here, for example, are outlined the choices you have in a familiar type of case.

You have just learned that a good friend is seriously ill and is facing a possible operation within the next couple of weeks. You immediately have the following choices, among others:

1. To get in touch right away.
2. To wait until the operation has been completed and then send a "Get Well" card.
3. To get more information and think about it.
4. To do nothing.

If you decide to communicate, then you have to choose whether to:

1. Make a phone call.
2. Write a letter or card.
3. Visit in person.

4. Relay your concern through a third party.
5. Communicate through some other medium.

If you choose to take some form of action, the procedure does not stop with these decisions because now you have to decide what you will say. Suddenly, words become very important. You balk at saying "I'm sorry" and making it seem as though you realize that the situation is very serious. Yet you also do not want to sound as though you are taking the matter too lightly.

Start making a list of **"Choice Words"** that relate to the various people and subject areas with which you are most concerned. Over a period of time, you will find this list very helpful as a way in which you improve your communications and relate to other people. Use words that are clear, strong, and forceful and avoid those that are weak, indecisive, and soggy. Scrap words that are long and confusing and substitute ones that are short and perky. Here are some examples of words that can enhance your ability to communicate:

able	crave
admirable	crotchety
adroit	crusty
agile	demure
applaud	dexterity
ardent	dire
arrogant	disquieting
astute	eternal
baneful	exacting
beguiling	exquisite
bewitching	fellowship
blessed	fluid
blustery	fountain
brisk	glistening
caustic	glow
chasten	graceful
cherish	harbor
citadel	impending
compelling	implore
coy	incandescent

intrepid
kindle
lofty
luster
merit
mischief
nimble
persuasive
prevalent
princely
quicksand
quiver
radiant
relish
renegade
reticent
ruse
rustic
saucy
searching
singular

skirmish
snappy
snug
sparkling
splendor
spry
strive
supple
tart
teeming
testy
towering
unceasing
unfailing
urgent
vacation
veer
vigilant
wit
zest

Make lists of words you like and that do something for whatever message you are trying to communicate. At the same time, list the meaningless, trite, or overworked words and phrases you would like to avoid. The following are examples of what you might want to pare from your vocabulary:

acid test
along the lines of
bitter end
cute
due to
few and far between
furthermore
I want to thank
inasmuch as
leaps and bounds
likewise
nice

on account of
prior to
quick as a flash
with a view to
with regard to
yours truly

You will be able to choose your words more carefully and make them more effective and memorable if you will buy and use a thesaurus from time to time. A thesaurus is defined as "a book of systematically classified words with their synonyms and often their antonyms," (words that are *alike* in meaning and *opposite* in meaning.) Thesauruses are not only (1) published as books, but (2) programmed into computers and (3) produced as instruments that resemble calculators. Every time you feel that you are overworking a word, using it incorrectly, or would be better off with a synonym, refer to your thesaurus and select a substitute that is stronger, clearer, or more witty.

The choice is yours.

Index